How I Married Michele

and other journeys

Also by Gary Gildner

Poetry
Cleaning a Rainbow
The Bunker in the Parsley Fields
Clackamas
Blue Like the Heavens: New & Selected Poems
The Runner
Nails
Digging for Indians
First Practice

Limited Editions
The Birthday Party
The Swing
Pavol Hudák, the Poet, Is Talking
Jabón
Letters from Vicksburg
Eight Poems

Fiction
The Capital of Kansas City
Somewhere Geese are Flying: New & Selected Stories
The Second Bridge
A Week in South Dakota
The Crush

Memoir
My Grandfather's Book: Generations of an American Family
The Warsaw Sparks

Anthology
Out of this World: Poems from the Hawkeye State

How I Married Michele
and other journeys

Essays

GARY GILDNER

BkMk Press
University of Missouri-Kansas City

BkMk Press
University of Missouri-Kansas City
5101 Rockhill Road
Kansas City, MO 64110

Executive editor: Christie Hodgen
Managing editor: Ben Furnish
Assistant managing editor: Cynthia Beard

Partial support for this project has been provided by the Missouri Arts Council, a state agency.

For a complete list of donors, see page 247.

"Playing Cath with My Daughter" from *The Bunker in the Parsley Fields.* © 1997 by Gary Gildner, reprinted with permission of the University of Iowa Press.

"Letter to a Substitute Teacher," "First Practice," and "My Father After Work" from *Blue Like the Heavens: New and Selected Poems* by Gary Gildner. © 1984. Reprinted by permission of the University of Pittsburgh Press.

Library of Congress Cataloging-in-Publication Data

Names: Gildner, Gary, author.
Title: How I married Michele : essays / Gary Gildner.
Description: Kansas City, MO : BkMk Press, [2021] | Summary: "These fifteen personal essays describe the author's significant journeys, whether across the world to such locations as Czechoslovakia, Poland, or from his native Michigan to Iowa and rural Idaho, or across time to consider his Polish-German family's immigrant story, his friendships with writers such as Raymond Andrews and Richard Hugo, his coming of age as a student in Michigan Catholic schools and as a poet and writer, husband, and father"-- Provided by publisher.
Identifiers: LCCN 2020056065 | ISBN 9781943491223 (paperback)
Subjects: LCGFT: Essays.
Classification: LCC PS3557.I343 H69 2021 | DDC 814/.54--dc23
LC record available at https://lccn.loc.gov/2020056065

ISBN: 978-1-943491-22-3

This book is set in Cambria.

Contents

Acknowledgments

These essays first appeared in the following publications:

The Georgia Review: "Ray," "Something Clear and True," "Dick Hugo's Green Sport Coat" and "Tearing Down the Barn."

The Massachusetts Review: "Six Fat Paragraphs."

New Letters: "Juventútem Meam," "Looking Out," "Journeys We're On," and "Stealing."

The New York Times Magazine: "Closer."

North American Review: "Street Smart."

The Review of Contemporary Fiction: "Fact and Fiction With Konwicki" (under the title "I Am Invited to Write About Konwicki").

The Southern Review: "Where the Dog Is Buried" and "How I Married Michele."

Confrontation: "A Very Small Cemetery."

Parts of two or three essays found their way into my memoir, *My Grandfather's Book: Generations of an American Family* (Michigan State University Press, 2002).

"Where the Dog is Buried" received a Pushcart Prize, "Juventútem Meam" a Pushcart Special Mention. "How I Married Michele" and "Looking Out" received Notable honors in *The Best American Essays* series.

for Michele

How I Married Michele

make something from the
skein unwinding, unwinding
something I could wear

or something you could wear
when at length I rose to meet you

—Denise Levertov

The first day of class she sat in the front row, but that was too close, she told me almost thirty years later. So at the next meeting she moved to the last row.

"I don't remember you in the first row," I said.

"It was all girls—constantly crossing their legs."

"You didn't like sitting with girls?"

"The whole class was girls. There was one guy. Maybe three."

"So?"

"You never once used the lectern. You paced."

"This bothered you?"

"Let's just say farther away was better."

What I remember: all semester she never raised her hand, never said a word. She agreed this was true. I went out to the garden and gathered some tomatoes and chard, thinking about it. When I came in for lunch, I said, "I'm curious. Why did you really take the class?"

"I love poetry."

"Which is why you went to law school?"

"Objection."

At the final exam, she reminded me, I told the students to write an essay on anything they wanted.

"'Just make it interesting,' you said."

"Didn't I suggest connecting it to poetry?"

"Anything we wanted, you said."

"I was hopeful."

"Hopeful about getting away to Paris with that trite blonde."

"How do you know?"

"I know."

Michele is a redhead, exactly five feet tall, but she seems taller. She has excellent posture, thanks to ten years of ballet. From six to sixteen she worked under the demanding Madame Tatiana Dokoudovska, whose Russian blood and smile were both thin and icy. Michele's legs were beautiful—and still are—but finally not long enough to satisfy Dokoudovska. Moreover, her breasts had become voluptuous. "Enough!" the Russian declared, dismissing Michele from her passion.

In high school she played her flute (first chair) and, as a cheerleader, stood atop a pyramid of girls, her arms thrown out imploring the Raytown Bluejays to fight, and then she flew off toward the football field or basketball floor in a somersault.

"Caught by the other cheerleaders?"

"Usually I landed on my own, in a roll."

"You were a tough cookie."

"A dramatic cookie."

"You struck me as shy."

"I was a shy, dramatic cookie."

The cheerleading lasted one year. She quit when her best friend asked her to, so that the friend could take her place.

"Seems odd for a friend."

"It meant a lot more to her than it did to me."

Her English teacher, Maryfrances Wagner, a poet, fed Michele's love of reading. They became friends, the teacher inviting the student to family gatherings. An Italian family. Exuberance, food, color. A big change from the more measured Episcopalian rhythms and rather bland dishes of home.

Maryfrances encouraged her to write poems. This led to Michele entering a writing competition sponsored by the Kansas City Jewish Community Center. The poet Denise Levertov came to town to give a reading at the center and judge the competition finalists. Michele's entry received first place in the high-school division.

"Would you let me read your poem?"

"It's packed away."

"What's it about?"

"The man under my bed."

"The man under your bed?"

"Yeah. He steals my Oreos and reads my mail."

"And?"

"It's a stupid, smart-ass poem. All the poems I wrote in high school were stupid and smart-ass."

"Why are you mad?"

"I can tell good from bad."

"Maryfrances and Levertov thought your stuff worthy."

"Crap, take my word."

I know Maryfrances. We met years ago when a college in Missouri invited her, Larry Levis, and myself to be part of a workshop for high-school English teachers who wanted to learn more about poetry—especially contemporary poetry—and ways to approach it with their students. I remember Maryfrances's enthusiasm in engaging the teachers, how articulate and gifted she was—far more than Larry or I—at supplying the kinds of exercises they were seeking. She helped them not only with pedagogy but also with their confidence.

Over the years, when visiting in Kansas City, giving readings there, I have sat down to many tasty meals at which Maryfrances and her husband Greg Field, also a poet, were present.

When she learned that Michele was taking my poetry class at Drake—a reading course, not writing—she sent me a note. I was in for a treat, she said.

"And yet, not a peep from that back row."

"I did invite you over for dinner. Properly. After the class was finished. I even came to get you, so you wouldn't have to bicycle after dark."

"I don't think I ever told Maryfrances about that dinner."

"I was *trying* to seduce you."

"If only your cat hadn't jumped on me. Right in the crotch. A real—"

"It wasn't Malcolm, it was the fish. God, what a botch."

"You've gotten much better in the kitchen. In fact . . ."

"Are we hesitating?" she said.

"We are reaching for the truest word, the highest compliment."

"Oh, well."

"I love your cooking. It's as good as, and sometimes even better than, my mother's—and *she* was superb."

"Thank you. Raising two boys certainly helped."

"Whenever I saw Maryfrances, she gave me your news."

"Didn't scare you?"

"After you drove me home, I'd remember how we sat on my kitchen floor, having a nightcap."

"Was I wearing a short, tan skirt?"

"You were."

"I kept waiting."

"I'm sorry. I really am."

"You had that blank blonde on your brain."

"Only part of my brain. The small part that resembles a crab apple."

"I'm going to forgive all that. And the overcooked fish."

Decades went by. We each survived our successes and mistakes, our good luck and not so good. Michele lived most of that time in mostly hot, humid Tulsa. To ease the pain, she jokes—but is not joking—she did civil-rights work.

"I was told that as late as the 1960s a Black police officer in Oklahoma could not arrest a white person. Talk about—about what? Something unwritten but enforced. Anyway, we finally got the Black cops on equal footing with the white cops."

At the other end, the firm she worked for also represented Oklahoma's prisoners in a suit against the state over poor living conditions: being housed in cells that had been condemned, for example. This was a two-decade battle, started in 1972. When she joined the fight, in 1996, they went all the way to the US Supreme Court, Michele writing the briefs.

"The lead plaintiff in the suit was named *Bobby Battle*."

"You wouldn't make that up."

"I couldn't. And guess what—we won."

One night I woke up, all wet, under a full moon filling the skylight over my bed. I felt I needed to explain something to her before I died. First thing in the morning, I called Maryfrances, who relayed my message. The next night Michele called, and said:

"Where *are* you? Are you okay?"

"Idaho. I'm okay. Where are you?"

"Mississippi."

"Mississippi?"

"Jackson. Home of Eudora Welty. A *huge* billboard reminds us."

"Why Mississippi?"

"Depositions. Tons of depositions. I just found an email from Maryfrances—she says you need to tell me something."

"I had this dream."

"Thank God. I thought you'd been in an accident, were dying."

"I was soaking wet."

"What happened?"

"I don't know, exactly. Inexactly, I was worried I'd never see you again."

"It's been almost thirty years."

"Twenty-seven."

"A girl can't wait forever."

"I know."

THAT SPRING, AS I APPROACHED Tulsa, it was hot and humid. I was driving a pickup without air, following the arrows I had made on an old road map. The map said that Oklahoma's state flower was the mistletoe, a plant I usually associated with snow and kissing. I remembered that Mickey Mantle, Woody Guthrie, Will Rogers, and Wilma Mankiller, the Cherokee chief, all came from Oklahoma. The great Jim Thorpe too, winning those Olympic gold medals, having them taken away. I also remembered seeing in *Look* the sequence of photos showing an Oklahoma A&M defensive tackle approach the visiting Johnny Bright, a Black player carrying the football for Drake and, at that moment, leading the nation in rushing. I was in junior high. Instead of trying to tackle Bright (a good-looking young man, by the way), the defender gathered his hands into fists—in the photos you can see this developing—and broke Bright's jaw, stopping a most probable brilliant season.

Later I taught at Drake. In 1971 the university gave John Berryman, author of *The Dream Songs*, an honorary degree, strangely the only one, among all his honors, that he ever received. The day before, he wanted to visit the Des Moines Art Center, and I took him there. When he came to Courbet's *Valley of the Loue*, he sat on the floor before it. He sat there, cross-legged, almost thirty minutes without moving. In the picture, dominated by a mountain, you can make out a trail up the side and on the trail—about halfway to the top—probably a traveler. I have looked at that painting many times and I have always seen a traveler, not just a small dark smudge suggesting a figure. So here's the question: Is he going up the mountain, that is, advancing his journey, seeking the heights; or is he coming down—satisfied, disappointed, exhausted? Or is he hesitating en route, frozen?

Berryman was born in McAlester, home of Oklahoma's largest prison, where the state's executions take place; over the next ten years of his life, young John lived in Anadarko, Lamar, Sasakwa, and Wagoner, towns seldom on the tips of the tongues of most Oklahomans. His father was a banker, his mother a teacher. Then the family moved to Florida, where only moments, it seemed, before John would become a teenager, the banker walked off to where the ocean rolled in and shot himself dead, his son watching. (You can read a response to this act in the penultimate *Dream Song*.) Six months after receiving the Drake honorary degree, Berryman leaped to his death from a Minneapolis bridge, his pockets emptied of all identification except for a blank check.

IN MY CONTEMPORARY POETRY COURSE, I often read aloud from *The Dream Songs*:

> Bats have no bankers and they do not drink
> and cannot be arrested and pay no tax
> and, in general, bats have it made.
> Henry for joining the human race is *bats*.

Though he denied it up, down, and sideways, Berryman is most likely Henry, the narrator and main character of this long sequence of 385 poems. He is witty, sad, mad, outrageous, brilliant, lustful, learned, sorry, and more. At times fun to be with, at times a bore. He himself says so. He never says he is only a small dark smudge, not exactly. I could go on and on, trying to figure things out, as I often did in that poetry course Michele eventually took, leaving the front row to ponder quietly from the back.

Just plain old remembering, though, is sometimes rich enough. I like to remember, for example, when my daughters were born and how they later curled in their favorite corners to read, my mother's kitchen and how happy my father was to sit at her table, that fish dinner Michele still rolls her eyes over. I like to remember the sunny, sweet-smelling pine morning in May when we held hands going down the courthouse steps, the Clearwater Mountains, the South Fork rushing through them when we've been away and are now on our way back.

Juventútem Meam

The light ring roused me enough to pick up the phone beside my bed. A woman said my name and then hers so warmly I let her go on: her mother—Patricia, did she say?—had just died, and in a few minutes the woman on the phone would be leaving Pennsylvania and heading for Michigan.

"The funeral is Friday."

"What happened?"

The caller, Donna, said her mother had gone into the hospital with a nagging flu and died there of an aneurysm.

"All very unexpected. Except for that virus, she was in good health. I wanted to call because Mom was always very fond of you."

"How old was she?" I said, waking up more.

There was a pause. Then: "This *is* the Gary Gildner who went to Holy Redeemer in Flint?"

"Yes."

"She was your age."

I snapped fully awake. She was talking about my high-school girlfriend.

"I am so sorry," I said.

"I woke you up, didn't I?"

Where I lived in northern Idaho was, as a matter of fact, on Pacific time, I said. "But, really, it's okay."

Donna said she would back up. She reminded me of when we'd met: in the mid-1980s at Michigan State while I was visiting writer there and she was a student. She'd come to my office. Her mom, actually, had sent her to meet me. Donna now lived in Bucks County and had two boys who loved baseball.

Here's what she knew: at the hospital, an infectious disease doctor pressed on Patricia's abdomen when she was not very alert and she screamed. Her own doctor came in later and also pressed on her abdomen, causing her to scream even worse. Nothing was done right away. They were thinking *diverticulitis* and wanted to wait for things to calm down; they waited too long.

Because she was on blood thinners, bleeding internally all this time, there was, finally, nothing anyone *could* do. She died of an abdominal aortic aneurysm. Patricia was a nurse, she had worked lots of ERs, assisted at heart operations, and near the end of her career served as head nurse in a chronic pain clinic. How was this scenario of screams-leading-to-nothing-anyone-could-do possible in a hospital? Screams by one of their own? Donna said her mother's Mass would be at Holy Redeemer at eleven o'clock on May 8th, the day after tomorrow.

The second phone call I got that morning, after a shower and coffee, was from my publisher, to tell me that a poem from my new collection was going to be read on public radio's the *Writer's Almanac* in a couple of weeks. "Rock Tea," the poem, is about (to put it simply) the journey of life.

I was dumbfounded at Patricia's death, and angry. But neither bewilderment nor anger could compete with the images that started rushing into my head: among which, not oddly, were some nuns we'd known who could briskly enter a classroom and immediately render us mute, alert, servile, ready to scale a wall, scared, happy, nervous, confident. All more or less at once. They wore the full habit in those days—Holy Cross sisters from South Bend—and they wore it to win. The only time they lost control was when the pastor, Father Louis P. Gauthier, short and round, rolled into class like Napoleon because he had been inspired, suddenly, to share some of his thoughts.

He left English, math, and biology alone, but religion and history and Latin were his for the taking, since they were so solidly in his bailiwick and, anyway, always good backdrops for the largesse he was eager—beaming—to distribute.

"If Sister doesn't mind?"

She never did, of course. How could she, committed as she was to poverty, chastity, and obedience? Forget that the wedding ring-like band on her third finger symbolized a spiritual hip to hip with J.C. himself. He couldn't help her, *nicht wahr?*

And what were Father's enthusiasms? A love of learning. Order. "Always," he would advise, "keep a pencil in your hand when you're reading a book. I do." And then we'd get to hear, once again, how he played saying Mass at the altar he'd built in the attic of his boyhood. *Ora pro nobis.* Pray for us, indeed.

Patricia's death took me back to that disciplined, conformist, but rich-in-introspection—sometimes wildly rich—parochial school theatre of our youth.

FOR HALF A DOZEN YEARS after World War II, Holy Redeemer consisted of grades one through eight. When my class achieved the eighth grade, Father Gauthier announced that the following year, 1952, HR would offer ninth grade, the year after that tenth, and so on until we were a complete high school. As a result, Patricia and I and our classmates were, in effect, "seniors" for five years.

This would be a potent state. Our egos and swagger, however, were greatly modified by Sister Good Counsel, who was brought in to be the architect—and first principal—of this new high school. Our previous principal, Sister Lenore, who made her sporty, angular way under that black wrapping neatly as a solved problem in geometry, was more at home on the playground, taking her cuts at the plate, than in laying down heavy academic challenges. Once, when she was pitching, I drove the fat softball straight back to the mound and broke her rather regal Roman nose—a blow that barely slowed her down. She shook it off with a laugh and a wave. Of course we all loved her.

Sister Good Counsel taught biology and could put icy Darwinian fear into our hearts just by looking at us through those immaculate rimless octagonal glasses that burned the dither off our guilt-trussed morphologies like the most powerful magnifiers ever. Without fanfare she let it be known, immediately, that Holy Redeemer High School would be offering only college prep courses. Latin, science, *all* the math. If any student wanted things like home ec or shop, he or she could go to a public school.

The previous year the HR boys had announced their presence with authority in handsome fashion pursuing the Knights of Columbus football championship. Now we were looking forward to creaming the Catholic high schools of Flint when we joined that competition in tenth grade. Here's where we *could* swagger. Sister Good Counsel's college prep agenda, however, sent half of that strutting eighth grade football team into the city's public school system. Those of us who remained learned to wear neckties and trousers (not wash pants, never jeans), and the girls were outfitted with maroon jumpers that hung like Lenten sackcloth on their budding figures.

Except for Jenny. She could be bundled in industrial-strength insulation and still show her precocious curves. At least once a week, it seemed, her name came through the intercom speaker that hung over the crucifix at the front of every classroom, asking her to report to the office. We all could guess that her jumper wasn't sufficiently draping—yet again—her actively advancing presentation.

Sex was of course everywhere: from the virgin-birth story and fruity underarm feminine scents at the north end of campus where the church rose up, to its southern tip, where the new high school was taking shape, the two scintillant points conjoined by a long polished *reflective* hallway at either end and down the distance of which one's fantasies could enrich themselves undisturbed behind the most pious of façades.

I was stimulated daily, starting with morning Mass, not least when holding the paten under the offered tongues of certain girls kneeling to receive the Host: *Take ye, and eat, for this is my body.*

I was stimulated in class when Jenny played a gold chain up and down inside her yellow blouse, easing it over and over into the valley of her (unseen but vividly imagined) cleavage, caressing herself as if in compensation for the onerousness of having to employ her hot-pink ink pen (whose phallic cap she would occasionally slip between her lips) at composing an essay.

I was stimulated when Constance ran her hands down that portion of maroon drape covering her shapely hams in preparation for sliding smoothly into her seat—and immediately crossing her legs—in algebra.

The list of stimulants may be almost endless.

Let me finish—at least for the moment—by singing the sweet name of Delphine Bononi, for many reasons, but principally in honor of a scene which took place at the precipice of my entrance into puberty. She raised her large purple eyes from assessing the latest developments in her already full, miraculous front and looked me long and frankly in the eye across the library table and the glistening reproductive works of the frog we had together, turning the pages of a book, just exposed. And how did I respond? I fell, of course, forward. A distance so great that even I, to this day, have trouble identifying my remains.

O Delphine, so evanescent and yet so there in this softly measurable, phenomenal meld, where did you disappear to?

Where, for that matter, did the rest of us go, the thirty-four survivors who filtered into the first college-prepared graduation class of Holy Redeemer High School?

IN FOURTH GRADE, WHERE MY HR memories begin, our teacher was Sister Macrina. Young, pretty, energetic, Sister Macrina also had charge of the altar boys, and fourth grade was when I joined up—or was conscripted. I don't remember how it happened, exactly, but I do remember, once in the ranks, enjoying the duty. I didn't even mind all that much serving at the five o'clock Sunday morning Mass attended mainly by drinkers and old women clad in the somber colors of grief—all of them kneeling, standing, and sitting in such tentative, fragile attitudes they might have been the last to escape a terrible war. Though as I got older, if I could get out of that hard hour, I would.

Sister Macrina enjoyed training her acolytes more than teaching fourth grade, I think. She loved the Latin language and the ceremony of the Latin Mass; when we achieved lyrical perfection in our memorized responses at the altar, choreographed well (moving more like Gene Kelly, less like Frankenstein, was good), *and* looked sharp—combed hair, crisply ironed surplice, shined shoes, and where that inch or two of trouser showed below the cassock, a smart break at the cuff—she was clearly a very happy, c'meer-give-us-a-hug-happy, young woman. Minus, just barely, the hug.

It became my aim in church to first make Sister Macrina happy, see her smile and blush from wherever it was she went inside. Would I have done anything she asked? Among my top five most erotic dreams was kissing her on the lips. To this day, if a priest started things off with *Introíbo altáre Dei* (I will go unto the altar of God), I could respond *Ad Deum qui laetíficat juventútem meam* (Unto God who giveth joy to my youth)—and deliver all the other responses in the Latin Mass, High or Low. Could deliver, that is, if there were such Masses anymore, and if I were not, as the phrase labels me, "fallen away."

All the ways you could fall away! Maybe the worst was by "keeping company" with a Protestant, slipping and sliding around among your "lower emotions." Next thing you know you're married to her or him, missing Mass, not making your Easter duty—boom!—you've lost your precious way.

I can still hear the visiting Irish priest, who sucked Tums for a sour stomach, pronounce the three syllables of *Protestant* as if his medicinal mint had suddenly surrendered the bitter taste of something foreign, like a fly. He came to HR to conduct a special retreat, boost our awareness in matters close to the heart of *hooley muther charch*. Theft, drunkenness, even murder were less dangerous to our immortal souls, it seemed, than keeping company with a Protestant. Just writing that last sentence releases remnants of the thrill I used to feel when barely flirting with the idea. A Protestant girl waiting around the next bend to seduce me? Did she have black hair and black eyes like Jenny? And could she walk like that? But I'm getting ahead of myself. Falling away hadn't come up yet.

What else do I remember from fourth grade? I remember the strange pale pigtailed presence of Diane P., whose father had been killed in the war, and who finished her assignments so fast—and thoroughly—she spent most of the day inventing crossword puzzles that challenged, rumor had it, even our own Sister Macrina. Diane never raised her hand for anything. Never said a word when called on or at any other time that we knew. She even preferred to sit silently at her desk than go out for recess. We knew she was not deaf and mute, because Sister continued to call on her, gently, smiling, sometimes teasingly, as if this were a little game between them. No dice. Not a return smile, not a peep. And Diane's behavior was made stranger by the fact that her mother was a teacher in the public schools. How could she not know better? She became so formidable at maintaining her perfect silence, inventing her puzzles, that she disappeared before anyone else and, as far as I know, for good.

I also remember Patricia in fourth grade. She was Patricia G. then. Dimpled, earnest and quiet, but not speechless. She wore thick glasses that enlarged her pretty eyes, though I would not notice they were pretty until much later. When her glasses slipped down her nose if only a fraction, she used the back of her index finger in a smooth, natural gesture to slide them back up, as if casually righting a wayward curl of hair. It took me a few years to notice this, too. She usually had the correct answer when called on. A little later she became Patricia C. when her mother remarried, and then, senior year—our true senior year—she became my girlfriend and salutatorian of our class, missing valedictorian by a sliver to Diane A.

Diane A. did not invent anything, certainly nothing as strange as crossword puzzles. Looking back, it's easy to see her as a first class example of the beau ideal student in those early postwar, Eisenhower years: she never stepped out of line, responded correctly enough times to gain the reputation of "a brain," got all As, and delivered a valedictory that said we could find true happiness by subordinating our ambitions to Him. A theme no doubt strongly influenced by good local counsel. Patricia's salutatory was equally pious.

DONNA HAD GIVEN ME HER phone number in Pennsylvania. About three weeks after the funeral, I called. I said I was sorry that time, distance, and a prior commitment prevented me from being there. She understood. Her mom's two best friends in Flint couldn't attend either—they were traveling abroad. It was a wonderful service, Donna said. The music was very moving, the priest dynamic, and everything went off as planned.

"Mom left detailed instructions—actually a book—of what she wanted. My brother and sisters and I followed them to a T."

I was not surprised at Patricia leaving such instructions.

"How many siblings do you have?" I asked Donna.

"My sister Kathy, then Tom—he's a teacher and coach—then Karalyn. I'm third, between Tom and Karalyn."

I knew Patricia had been married twice. Her first marriage was annulled, then she married a man a dozen years her senior. She told me this at our fortieth high-school reunion—the first one we had. She was shy revealing the annulment, her details scarce and somewhat fuzzy (perhaps because in school we'd been told that annulments were rare and basically meant an inability to consummate); what came through very clearly was her summary statement that the church had presented a few bureaucratic hurdles, but she was persistent. I could still hear her underlining *persistent*, the satisfaction in her voice at getting what she wanted. Then she changed the subject.

"Do you remember why I chose nursing?"

"We talked about that, didn't we?"

"You spoke very highly of it. And how close Kalamazoo was to East Lansing."

"Forty years ago," I said.

We hadn't seen each other since our freshman year in college, the formal dance at Nazareth she'd invited me to. "Our last date, Gary, because Kalamazoo and East Lansing weren't *that* close, after all."

She laughed, waving her hand as if shooing away forty years and the capriciousness of youth, letting me off the hook. She looked good that weekend: trim, vivacious, stylish. Still dimpled, but no glasses. Even her way with a cigarette enhanced her youthful attractiveness. Robert, her husband, wasn't with her, she said, because he was tired.

The morning Donna called me, she mentioned that her mom had lost Robert some years ago. I wondered what the daughter knew about that first husband who, qua husband, ceased to exist. I said to her, following my question about her siblings, "At our fortieth reunion, Patricia told me about her annulment."

"She didn't believe your class would *ever* have one!"

"A reunion? Nor did I. I think it had something to do with being 'seniors' for five years—and being so cocky. Does that make any sense?"

"No," she laughed.

"How about cocky *and* smart?"

Donna said, "Speaking of smart, Mom was always disappointed at not being valedictorian, losing the scholarship to Saint Mary's College. She blamed it on taking all the hard courses, while that other girl took some easy ones, like home ec."

I started to say something, stopped myself, then tried to get back to Patricia's marriages. "Anyway, I was wondering about when your mom married Robert, your dad."

"He wasn't my dad. My dad—*our* dad—was Mom's first husband."

"The father of all four of you?"

"Yes." She paused a beat. "He had a drinking problem."

Trust the genius of the church, I thought, to provide a way, after four children, to execute a divorce without calling it that.

And what was this about home ec?

A FEW DAYS LATER I WAS tilling the raised beds of my vegetable garden when I remembered a box of school stuff my mother had insisted I take off her hands. She was too old, she said, to keep track of my junk anymore. I found the box in my studio: scrapbooks, yellowed sports clippings from the *Flint Journal,* copies of the *Beacon*, HR's first student newspaper, photos, three gold *R* varsity letters I never had sewn on any sweater or jacket.

I also found a folder of assignments, graded "O.K.," from typing class. Of course we had typing—so that in college we could neatly type up our term papers. I hadn't forgotten that course; I just never included it among Sister Good Counsel's academic offerings because in her point system it didn't amount to much: an ability to type, though useful, hardly exercised the mind.

Searching in the box, I came up with the June 1, 1956 issue of the *Beacon*—the year's final, our graduation issue—and a class history by Deanna. It supported my memory of Sister Good Counsel's program pretty well, except for one detail. "In September of 1954," Deanna wrote, "when the high school enrollment totaled 185, the commercial courses were added. Would-be secretaries and accountants were pleased with the inclusion in the curriculum of shorthand, typewriting, and bookkeeping."

Ah, our principal relaxed, relented, and retreated a bit. I'd forgotten all that. But was her decision surprising? The freshman and sophomore classes behind us were loaded—surely satisfying to our pastor—but in the practical-minded 1950s, especially in blue-collar Flint, not a few parents must have asked this question: What were their daughters going to do with all that science and Latin when their sights were aimed at Comptometer School in Flint?

On the same page as Deanna's history there is a story titled "Pastor Sees 19 Seniors to College," accompanied by a photo. There we are, nineteen smiling HR Flyers, gathered just outside the school's main portal, waving goodbye to Louis in his cassock and biretta. Yes, I remembered setting up this picture and assigning someone to compile the list of college-bound. I was the *Beacon's* editor, for God's sake!

Of those nineteen heading off to college, fifteen said they were staying home to attend Flint Junior College (7), Burroughs Comptometer School (3), nursing programs at local hospitals (3), General Motors Institute (2). Three of us announced we were leaving town—but not the state—for the University of Detroit (Bob), Nazareth College of Nursing in Kalamazoo (Patricia), and Michigan State (me). Diane's scholarship to Saint Mary's would take her all the way to South Bend, Indiana.

Twelve of the remaining members of that first graduation class said they would be seeking employment in Flint (most likely in an auto plant: GM was selling lots of cars in 1956) and three were joining the army. Two of the latter, Lenny and Dick, had worked summers in an upscale grocery store, and one summer they recommended me for a checker's job. Whenever we were assigned adjacent aisles, they'd say something to me like, "Check us out. Let us know if you see anything funny." Then they'd laugh. I never noticed a thing out of line.

Did I take notice of the fact that so many of us chose to remain so close to home? I don't remember. Myself, I was eager to get out of industrial Flint; and though the green campus in East Lansing was vastly, excitingly, refreshingly different, it was still only fifty miles away.

MORE IMAGES: SERVING AT A wedding Mass, I watch the kneeling groom's face turn paler and paler. I know he's going to faint and he does, falling back as if in slow motion, cracking his head open, his blood bright as the carnation in his lapel. The mother at her child's funeral throwing herself over the small white casket, calling God a liar, screaming to blow breath back in her baby's lungs. I wake some nights soaking wet, my mind racing. A gala fistfight. A kiss. Those Monday night Devotions to Mary, followed by bingo in the school cafeteria. *Oh-10! B-17!* Turkey raffles, paper drives, the summer festival and its mix of carnies and locals, the swirling scents of cotton candy and oily exhaust from the Whip, the Tilt-A-Whirl, and the parish ladies' jams and jellies, their warm fruit pies for sale.

HR had come a *long* way, people said, from those first makeshift Sunday services in the Burton Theatre. Now look. A stone-and-brick church and school, on all that land! Yes, the parish was certainly growing. Father Gauthier needed help.

Young assistants came and stayed a year or so, gaining experience, then went off to run their own parishes. "Business is good," one of them joked to us. Then there were the much older priests that Father Gauthier took in, word went, because they had nowhere else to go.

One of these refugees, I remember, was always smiling. Always. We preferred him for confession to anyone else, because we thought he didn't really understand us and therefore never gave more than three Hail Marys or three Our Fathers as penance. He was German and bald and stooped over, and his crooked fingers looked like roots. For recreation, he grew tomatoes behind the rectory garage. He never wore street clothes, just the black soutane. Never drove a car or had little jokes for the altar boys before Mass or ever really talked with us. It was the English, we said. Yet he seemed delighted with everything, even with saying, week after week, the five o'clock Sunday morning Mass. He always had the longest line waiting for him at Saturday confessions and got through it fast. We laughed about that. We went to him with our worst sins. We figured everybody did.

The priest Father Gauthier took in who stayed the shortest time had been a chaplain overseas. A big man, handsome, quiet. One weekday before Mass, just as we were preparing to leave the sacristy and begin, he spotted my open duffel bag in a corner and the football inside.

"You're the quarterback?"

I said I was. He bent down in his vestments and took the ball out and began fitting it to his hand, the way you do, almost caressingly. It was the first time I'd seen him smile. He raised his arm, holding the ball aloft as if he meant to throw it. I believed he might. Then he bent his knees, as if getting into position behind the center, and stepped quickly back, cocking his arm. He did this several times: he was trying to get everything right. Each time I believed more strongly that he might let the ball fly. He seemed happier and happier, improving his movements.

"Here," he said, "show me your grip."

I did. He nodded. Then he took the ball back, to show me where he used to place his hand. "Then I developed this new way." For ten or fifteen extraordinary minutes—the nuns and students in the pews no doubt wondering *what* was wrong—we traded the ball back and forth and admired our grips on it, how we could get the best spiral, how we held the ball when it rained or snowed. All this time, the other altar boy, Edward, said nothing, but his expression was of total disapproval. I never knew what to think about Edward, whether he was a stuffed shirt in the making or had been one from birth.

Sister Ambrozine, our fifth-grade teacher, was a very large woman with a perpetually red pebbly face, small voice, small white hands, and a crack between her teeth that produced a whistle on her sibilants. I remember almost nothing else from fifth grade and was glad when it was over. As an adult I have dreamt I needed to get to school early in the morning because Sister Ambrozine would be giving us a test in running, getting away, bunching our bodies in a crouch at the start of a race. She was probably more unhappy than I was, especially under all that black wool when Michigan turned hot and humid. But who knows?

I do know that the next year I received a startling love letter—my first ever. I was sitting at my desk in the row by the windows, gazing at the playground, probably wishing I was out there. When I stopped being dreamy and turned my attention to the room, I saw an envelope on my desk addressed to me. I opened it. Inside was a slip of paper that said: "T.S.T.S.T.S.A." I had no idea what that meant. So when I got the chance I made inquiries, causing, I noticed, several girls to titter. It finally came out that those capital letters meant "To Someone Too Sweet To Sleep Alone."

Years later, right after college, I was working in Detroit; my girlfriend, a grad student in theatre at Wayne State University, came home one time from spending the day in the inner city and showed me something she found among her books. It was a long, rambling, almost incoherent love letter. Carolyn had a teacher's certificate and would often substitute to supplement her scholarship. This letter she showed me came from a sixth grader, who was trying to say a difficult thing: how he felt. Reading his frantic run-on sentences, I recalled my sixth-grade love missive.

At the time I was writing a first novel and wanted to shoehorn this inner-city boy's passion into it. But I wasn't able to. Much later, when I was making poems, I put his experience and mine together—conflating us into one speaker—and wrote "Letter to a Substitute Teacher."

> Dear Miss Miller,
> You are someone
> too sweet to sleep alone
> and I can't help myself
>
> sitting here hearing
> your soft voice so

I must tell you
I like you

very much and would like
to know you better.
I know there is a difference
in our age and race

but we do have something
in common—You're a girl
and I'm a boy
and that is all

we need. Please
do not look at me
like I'm silly or sick
and most of all

please do not reject
my very first love
affair. If you do
not feel the same

as I do please
tell me how I can forget
your unforgettable voice
that reminds me

of Larry the Duke's pet
birds in the morning,
your blue eyes like the
Blessed Virgin's,

your golden hair and your
nice red mouth. Please
give me some sign
of how you feel.

I would rather be hurt
than forgotten forever.
Sincerely yours,
The Boy in the Green Shirt.

MY BEST FRIEND GROWING UP did not attend HR; Eddie Hill went
to Bendle, and he wants to jump in here before I get too far
along. Our houses sat back to back, separated by large yards, a
white picket fence, and, running along the fence on my side,
two lush rows of Concord grapevines whose produce my mother
turned into jelly every summer. Once, Eddie cleared both vines
and fence in a leap that no boy in his right mind, in tennis sneaks,
in the dark, exposing his jewels to such danger, would ever try.

We'd been hiding under my front porch with our BB guns
loaded with buckshot, waiting for some action, when a Burton
Township police car came down the street. I promised to open
fire on it when it came to a certain point. I was only kidding, of
course. I *was* planning to shoot, but only at the grass in front
of us. Eddie didn't know that. When the cruiser arrived at point
zero, he knocked my barrel up and into perfect position for a
direct hit.

Pit-pit-pit-pit-pit-pit.

The cruiser braked, spun its spotlight our way. Eddie was
streaking ahead of me; he made that truly heroic leap without
hesitation. After slipping around the fence in a crouch, I couldn't
find him. Finally I knocked on his back door.

Mrs. Hill said, "Eddie? Oh, he's in bed. He's been asleep for
some time, I believe."

Eddie's parents were janitors at Bendle High School four
blocks away. On weekends, they dressed up in their Western
outfits and went to square dances that Mr. Hill was hired to call.
He even made records. He was a tall, slender, prematurely bald
man with a chronic sore back who, nonetheless, could make a
baseball curve or suddenly sink or float in a dipsy-doodle way
without spinning.

He taught Eddie to pitch, and Eddie taught me. We spent
hours, he and I, perfecting our throws, our fielding, and hitting
a small plastic Wiffle-like ball with broom handles to sharpen

our batting eyes. In cold weather we practiced our jumpers and hooks under the net nailed above his garage door. When snow arrived, we shot baskets at night in the Bendle gym that his dad would open for us. I spent many Saturday nights sleeping over at Eddie's when his parents went dancing and his older half-sister, Bev, went out with her boyfriend. The Bendle track coach and his family lived across the street from the Hills, and a few doors away lived Mr. Lamb, Bendle's superintendent, and his wife. The Lambs had a daughter named Mary.

Our neighborhood in Burton Township, at the southern edge of Flint, was largely blue-collar (lots of factory workers, a sprinkling of skilled craftsman like my carpenter father), with a fair number of teachers. Diane P., the puzzle-maker, lived a couple of blocks over with her teacher mom, and up the street from me lived Mr. and Mrs. Skellinger, both of whom taught at Bendle, and their kids Jerry and Ruth Ann. Ruth Ann and my baby sister, Gloria, were the same age and played together; I sometimes played with Jerry, who was one grade ahead of me, very smart, with a head of hair like Paderewski, my mother said, but not much of an athlete.

The most athletic game that Jerry and I played was darts: he had a huge board in his basement. Once, a little too fancy in my windup, I got Jerry in the shoulder. We were shirtless, as boys often were in the summer, and he was standing beside the board, waiting to retrieve my throws for his turn. He looked down at the dart sticking out of his shoulder—he seemed to be studying it, actually, as he would any new problem. Finally he erupted into a siren-like wail and disappeared upstairs. I didn't see him for weeks. After that incident, which was never mentioned, we only played his board baseball game that wasn't going to hurt anybody.

Until I got involved in sports at HR, Eddie Hill was my near-constant after-school companion, and starting when we were eleven, we played summer-league baseball together until we graduated. Baldy's Service, a gas station, sponsored us in Midget League that first summer, and we won the city championship, playing our final game in Atwood Stadium, home to the professional Flint Arrows—and several future Detroit Tigers. Eddie pitched. I played shortstop (having taken that position away from skinny Paul Krause, who grew up and filled out, ultimately performing brilliantly for the Minnesota Vikings and inducted into the Football Hall of Fame).

Another summer, in a doubleheader, playing for Colonial Cleaners, Eddie pitched a no-hitter in the first game. I threw one in the second. Thanks to his dad, we had a dazzling arsenal of pitches: roundhouse curves, inshoots, drops, knucklers. One time a guy who had briefly pitched for the Philadelphia Phillies was giving us a clinic and warned about throwing too many curves. Rely on your fastball and good location, he said, don't strain your arm. This was not advice we wanted to hear—not when we could make a batter look foolish reaching for one of our sliders.

The summer I turned sixteen I would pitch another no-hitter, this time playing American Legion ball. Scouts began to watch me, charting my pitches. Wanting to impress them, I tried to throw a no-hitter every game I started—which meant throwing a lot of balls using a lot of torque, when I should have been using my head more. Two years later I could throw maybe three innings before my arm started to hurt, almost audibly buzz.

My best friend at HR, until his family moved to another parish, was Patrick. Our classmates called us the Gold Dust Twins. Patrick and I actually did resemble each other physically, but more significantly, we showed up one day at school wearing—not by accident—gold-colored sweatshirts and burgundy cords. Then in seventh grade we tried out for the eighth-grade baseball team and made it, a feat that practically framed us in neon.

The team won the Knights of Columbus title and the coach—a volunteer from the parish—and his wife hosted a victory party for us in their home. They invited, as well, a number of eighth-grade girls. At one point these older girls, who, to Patrick and me, were almost grown women, organized a game of post office in the basement rec room.

I remember four things from seventh grade. One, Sister Veronica's art slides (she had been to Italy, with a camera, was crazy about the Masters—especially Michelangelo and his Sistine Chapel, his *David*—and worked all year trying to make us crazy about them too). Two, grabbing geeky Richard by his chicken's-neck and threatening to wring it, making him cry, when, lining up after recess, he lunged at my crotch. Three, winning the K of C baseball championship on a perfect squeeze bunt in our last game and our last at-bat, the final score 1-0. Four, being kissed behind the coach's furnace—French-kissed—by Charleen, who took her time teaching me how, and who later became a Sister of the Holy Cross.

"That's nothing," Eddie said when I told him about my first kiss.

Eddie was in many ways my most vivid teacher during those years stumbling up to and reeling away from puberty. He introduced me not only to the curveball but to rubbers and Eight-Page Bibles (Popeye, erect, mounting Olive Oyl, whose *pigtail* is erect; Li'l Abner finally bedding an astonished Daisy Mae; Blondie and Dagwood, Archie and Veronica, everyone in comics throbbing and thrusting)—to rum-soaked crook cigars and the best tool for scaling the perch and bluegills we caught: a beer cap nailed upside down on a piece of lath.

Eddie's pursuit of knowledge included his beautiful sister, Bev, who filled a room with, to us, exotic intoxicating perfume when passing through it—and who was even more honeyed in her motion than Jenny because she was older, more practiced. Like his mom, Eddie was frightened by thunder-and-lightning storms, though he got better about them with age, while she got worse. One stormy night when their parents were out, Bev let him climb into her bed: he took along the flashlight he'd been carrying, and when he was sure Bev had fallen back asleep, he tunneled under the covers and looked her over in detail, seeing things, he told me, you can't see in pictures.

Eddie and his mom, Cleo, loved jigsaw puzzles—they always had one in progress on a card table in the living room. They also loved popcorn and toast. They looked more like brother and sister than Eddie and Bev did, especially when Cleo dolled up in her frilly Western dress. My mother was very fond of him, because he was always polite, always removed his shoes whenever he came in my house, and thrice-praised whatever she gave him to snack on: while the goodie was being chewed, after it was gone, and when he was slipping back into his shoes. Of course, he knew exactly what he was doing to guarantee a steady supply of cookies and generous slices of pie.

HR and the much larger Bendle only played each other once when Eddie and I were in school: a practice baseball game on April 15, 1954—Holy Thursday, as it happened. Trying to stretch a double into a triple, I broke my leg sliding hard into the bag. I heard the bone snap: it was the sound you get breaking a green twig in the spring. The cast came off June 10. This is all I said about that game in a note in my scrapbook.

When Eddie graduated, he had at least three good offers to play college baseball. (His pitching arm stayed fit longer than mine did.) But accepting any one of them would have meant leaving Flint. He chose to stay home, take a job on the railroad, and marry his high-school sweetheart. I am glad to say that whenever I saw him and Betsy they seemed goofily happy. Popular as ever in the neighborhood, Eddie was elected to the Bendle School Board, a neat trick for a C student, I told him. He hunted, fished, and drove his train the short distance between Flint and the old tank plant in Grand Blanc, hauling auto parts. He died at fifty-seven. Betsy preceded him by more than a decade.

ON THE FIRST DAY OF what we thought would be our last year at Holy Redeemer, an announcement came over the intercom directing all the eighth-grade boys who were interested in playing football to meet after school in the bomb shelter. HR had done so well with Knights of Columbus baseball the previous spring that Father Gauthier now wanted to get us on the gridiron.

As before, he advertised one Sunday from the pulpit for a coach—this time a volunteer who knew about football—and he got a former Marine who had played Service ball. Our coach was short and stocky. He sucked a short cigar, and he got our attention—and held it—as well as any nun or Irish retreat priest on their best days. In a poem, I call him Clifford Hill; I chose the name for what it suggests and how it sounds and did not intend for it to point in any way to any Hills I have ever known.

So we gathered in the large space underneath the school—a thick-walled basement with a low ceiling, no windows, and doors made of heavy metal—that was called the bomb shelter because in fact it was one. Many schools had them. This period of which I speak, when even ordinary citizens were known to bury bunkers in their back yards and victual them, did not truly make the frightened, crazy aspect of its character known to us, or at least to me, until later.

I remember the summer that Bob and I answered a newspaper ad for construction work. We were in high school then, wanting to get in shape for football in the fall. Our employer—for one day—turned out to be a minister of God (that's what he told us) who sold home bomb shelters on the side. He needed strong young men like ourselves, he said, to dig the holes. What Bob and I would have helped this man plant in the Michigan earth, we soon saw, were nothing more than giant tin cans fit perhaps for stewed meats.

But the bomb shelter of our school was another matter. Lining up suddenly at a buzzer to file down there in good order, following the nuns whose large rosary beads hanging from their waists crackled and snapped gaily against their thighs as they stepped along, was fun, almost festive, a break from classroom routine. If the threat of anything deadly occupied our minds during these practice runs, it was more likely a tornado than a Cold War nuclear weapon. There were already plenty of bombs around, and, to borrow from Pogo, they were us. Just ask our retreat master.

The bomb shelter became another matter entirely after a doctor listened to our hearts and felt under our shorts and told us to cough, and then Clifford Hill ushered the doctor out and closed the door. Lining us up according to size—two lines—he made a speech unlike any we had ever heard. Patrick stood across from me in Cliff's design to slug away at and be slugged at in return—but not in the face, where outsiders (parents, nuns) might read what the Holy Redeemer boys had been up to.

Some of us, later, felt ashamed at hitting out like that—at being *moved* by Cliff's speech. But I know that many of us were more afraid to lose a game than to break a bone, and we all felt proud when, at the conclusion of that successful season, Father Gauthier took the team to a restaurant in Frankenmuth, just north of Flint, and treated us to all its famous chicken we could eat.

For years I tried to write a short story about that experience, but the attempts always sounded wrong, false. I was spending too many words on something that wanted to be quick: boom.

One day I decided to simply "list" the story's important elements. Except for one unnecessary word, the poem "First Practice" appeared.

> After the doctor checked to see
> we weren't ruptured,
> the man with the short cigar took us
> under the grade school,
> where we went in case of attack
> or storm, and said
> he was Clifford Hill, he was
> a man who believed dogs
> ate dogs, he had once killed
> for his country, and if
> there were any girls present
> for them to leave now.
>   No one
> left. OK, he said, he said I take
> that to mean you are hungry
> men who hate to lose as much
> as I do. OK. Then
> he made two lines of us
> facing each other,
> and across the way, he said,
> is the man you hate most
> in the world,
> and if we are to win
> that title I want to see how.
> But I don't want to see
> any marks when you're dressed,
> he said. He said, *Now.*

IN HIGH SCHOOL, PATRICK AND I played against each other after he transferred to St. Agnes. Whenever our eyes met—in a football, basketball, or baseball game—he would break into a big smile. We were still buddies, the smile said. He called me

Hodges, after Gil Hodges of the Brooklyn Dodgers, because Gil was part of my name. I called him *Happy Boy*. He went to a small Michigan college on a football scholarship; he earned Little All-American honors and married his college sweetheart, a tall, vivacious girl with an intelligent, generous laugh.

One weekend I was in Flint visiting my parents, and Patrick and his wife invited me over for dinner. Patrick had been hired as an assistant coach at a large public school in the city. He led me outside at one point and said his wife was threatening to leave him. Though I had just met her, I saw nothing in her manner to suggest unhappiness with him; indeed, I saw a campus beauty still congratulating herself on landing a handsome football hero. I said was he crazy?

"She doesn't want to settle down in Flint," he said with heavy sadness.

I remember laughing.

"But I can be a head coach here one day," he said. "And Flint's a good place to raise kids. You know that." He went on to complain that his wife, however, the daughter of career foreign service officers, wanted to see more of the world.

"She's got that travel bug. Hodges," he pleaded. "You've traveled. You know it's not that big a deal."

"Hey, I haven't gone that far yet. But I'm hoping to."

"She reads a lot. And you're a writer. You could reach her."

His desperation and sadness stopped me from laughing again.

"Please?" he said.

AT THAT FORTIETH CLASS REUNION, several of us were not there: the known dead, the missing, those who couldn't attend or chose not to; one of the latter, Lenny, a tough, quick guard on our football team, said he had gotten too fat and had trouble walking. Not even Dick, who played tackle beside him and joined the army with him and shared in the funny business I was challenged to spot at that grocery-store job all those years ago, could coax him away from his La-Z-Boy and TV. I could still see the two of them at a school dance or at somebody's party, wearing yet another new cashmere sweater, new pegged flannels, expensive shoes.

"How do you guys afford these things?" I used to ask, shaking my head.

Dick finally told me. He would be checking, Lenny unloading the customers' shopping carts. (The store thought it was more efficient for an employee to unload and set the items on the conveyor belt, by category, price clearly visible to the checker, rather than trust the customer to be orderly.) When a shopper arrived whose full cart included, on the bottom rack, say a large expensive item like a $20 ham, Lenny would hesitate just long enough for Dick to tally up and rip off the receipt. Then Lenny would announce the ham. Dick would add $20 to the receipt with the pencil that lay over his ear, mentally keeping track of all such additions not recorded by his machine and at the end of his shift pocket them. This upscale grocery, owned by brothers of Arab descent, liked to hire parochial school students, they told us, because of our famous discipline.

Most of those who came to the reunion didn't have far to travel. They saw each other often at Sunday Mass in the new, much bigger church the parish had built. (The old church was converted into a gym.) They worked on the annual pledge drives. They worked at the summer festival still making its profitable appearances on the field where I once broke Sister Lenore's nose, the men running a bingo tent, the women offering their fruit pies among the carny rides and chances to win a stuffed teddy bear. Some, like Edward, still assisted with the liturgy.

Ah, good old disapproving Edward. His dyspeptic expression throughout our reunion suggested that everything about it was fundamentally wrong. Perhaps Edward should have passed on a wife and children and become a retreat priest instead of a GM engineer. How had the God of Central Casting given such a man the task of helping to supply the American car-buyer, year after year, with a fresh dose of styling, leg room, and acceleration?

Constance, who married soon after graduation, produced the most kids—almost enough to field a baseball team. When she and her future husband were courting, he drove a spiffy new convertible and worked, as the expression went, "in the shops." He still worked there but no longer drove a spiffy car. Constance told me she had never been out of the state.

"Never?"

After a moment, she said, "No," her ambiguous smile curling somewhere between regret and pride. In ninth grade Happy Boy Patrick, the future Little All-American, had a profound crush on Constance. In those blushing days, he'd wanted *on the spot* to root and bloom—did bloom—in the reddest red whenever she looked his way. How perfect she would have been for him.

The reunion organizers arranged for a Friday night drinks-and-finger-food party at Joyce's house, to be followed by a fancy dinner Saturday night at a Burton eatery owned by a member of the parish. When those few of us who had left Flint arrived at Joyce's, the locals were already there, waiting to test us: one at a time we had to stand in the middle of a circle and name names. At my turn I drew only one blank: she turned out to be the girl I had dated before Patricia. How some people can change. When the others cheerfully shouted her name—*Marian!*—her eyes narrowed at me; she was not happy. In a moment, though, she roared, "Nancy! We called Nancy and guess what she *told* us?"

Like Constance, Nancy married soon after graduation—into a family of retailers of high-end meats. Around the time GM started moving big chunks of its operation out of Flint, sending unemployment and crime to higher and higher levels, the meat store moved to Florida. Nancy's first response to the reunion committee about joining the party was "maybe." When Marian and some others put in a follow-up call, Nancy said, alas, she had to take a rain check: she'd promised, you see, to give her grandchildren a balloon ride that weekend.

But Nancy wanted Marian and everyone else in Flint to know that the store was doing just great. In fact, they kept a picture of the whole family on the main display case, and their many good customers always looked at it and *always* mistook Nancy for her attractive oldest granddaughter. Yes, Nancy said, it was *amazing*, she hadn't changed one bit since high school. Not one bit. Marian raised her glass and said, "To beautiful-always-young-gotta-take-a-rain-check-Nancy!" Then, knowing that Nancy had been my girlfriend before *her*, Marian cut her eyes at me and smiled.

As for Jenny's eyes, they sparkled, bubbled, and still might get you in a big mess of trouble—and were the only reason I could name her as I went around the circle: over our forty-year separation she had evolved into the same heartbreaking shape—and hardline political stance—as her heavy-breathing hubby.

Our valedictorian was not present and no one knew where she was, not even the Saint Mary's College alumni office. Nor was Bob present. At the University of Detroit on a football scholarship, Bob warmed the bench for four years but earned his BA—which may or may not have saved him from Vietnam during those early "police-action" years. Conscripted, he was sent to Fort Sill, Oklahoma, to produce lists of underwear and socks, putting to good, practical use his early manual typewriting training at HR and the polish he received from the Jesuits as an English major. In letters to me from Fort Sill he said what kept him from going crazy was taking up mountain climbing in

Oklahoma on his leaves. Mountain climbing in the home state of Woody Guthrie, Will Rogers, and Mickey Mantle?

As it happened, Bob and I had found ourselves going through our army physicals at the same time. Then I got a deferment to pursue an MA. Mrs. Brown, the classic little old lady on our draft board in Flint, said she would be waiting—enthusiastically: she planned to appoint me proctor of the bus taking the new boys down to Fort Sill, because she'd never had anyone like me before. How could I tell her that my future MA in comparative literature, in a crisis on the bus, would only result in de mal en pis? Add to this the news that Vietnam was heating up, and down in Fort Sill my friend Bob would be dutifully typing away, his letters reported, when his supply sergeant would sneak up behind him and for fun click his service pistol in Bob's ear.

All these things encouraged me to apply for admittance into the PhD program at Wayne State. At the last minute I was accepted. After one week, however, looking at myself in the mirror, I knew that I really didn't want a PhD. I wanted to write my novel.

I stopped going to class. More decisive, I never again went downtown to the Federal Building and declared, with a signature, that I was sitting up straight and being a good boy. That was around the time Carolyn showed me the love letter she'd received from her inner-city sixth-grader: his passion sustained me. It was also around the time Patrick asked me to convince his wife that Flint was the great, good place. I'd already made a smart decision (to stop the PhD nonsense and write my novel), so now I could afford a dumb one: I talked with Happy Boy's wife and promoted an exciting life with him in Flint, all the while, inside, siding with her instincts to get out of town. About a year later she did.

At the reunion, Constance said to me, when Patrick's name came up, "My mom told me he used to drop by her house and talk for hours. She said he was such a nice boy. He was, wasn't he?" Bob, after serving his time in the Sooner State, tried social work in northern Michigan, then became a university librarian in St. Paul. He also married a redhead, as I eventually did.

For the record, I never got to proctor the boys on the bus going down to Fort Sill—or anywhere. I like to think that Mrs. Brown had seen enough young men in Flint go off to die in a pointless war and lost her enthusiasm for me as a novelty. Also for the record, Patricia tied Deanna for salutatorian honors, but because Deanna took so many business courses Sister Good Counsel gave the higher nod to Donna's mom; she named Deanna class historian, a neat inter nos solution all around. Following Bob, who graduated fourth, came quiet Judy, who would study med tech at JC; then tomboyish Mary Jean and I tied for sixth. At the reunion Mary Jean, like Patricia, looked wonderful. Several of us told her so. She laughed and thanked us, sounding even more attractive. One of the highlights of the reunion—for me— was when I saw the former awkward tomboy passing a mirror and spontaneously give herself a quick wink, as if she had been right—or right enough—about her life for some time. I'll bet she slept very well that night. Kay was eighth, another quiet one, Madeline, ninth, and the ever-youthful Nancy tenth.

What does any of this mean, finally? Kay married Chester, Betty married his twin, Lester, and they all went into the tile and terrazzo business. Madeline quietly took her ninth-place finish to where no one could find her. Sister Good Counsel, we heard, had left the order. Now that was news, although exactly why it was news no one wanted to say, exactly. Some mysteries in this often-wondrous swirl are not meant for us to unwrap. After all our kneeling and supplicating, didn't we know that? It's almost like asking why so many of that first class chose to travel with ambitious Caesar in Gaul, in all three parts and in his own demanding tongue, and then elect to hunker down in familiar, reassuring, safe ground, even when it wasn't. Isn't.

In 1970 Holy Redeemer, along with all the other parishes in Flint that had them, gave up its high school to a new Catholic central called Powers. On May 29, 2009, due to a lack of interest, HR closed the door to its remaining eight grades—for good, the pastor, Father Tim MacDonald, announced exactly three weeks after he buried Patricia.

I first saw *The Maltese Falcon* my freshman year at Michigan State. This was not long after I managed the seventy-five miles to Kalamazoo and danced with Patricia on what turned out to be our only date that year and last ever. I told her, dancing, that I did not want to go back to Flint when we got our degrees. I was reading Whitman, Kerouac, Hemingway—I wanted to be a writer, see things, fall on my face if I had to.

Leaving the MSU Union, where the Bogart film had been shown, I heard a coed ahead of me say to another coed, "You're a good man, sister!" I admired and cheered Patricia's determination to be a good nurse, but I did not share in the precision her views took of what we needed to do to achieve a good, useful life. I didn't know nearly enough to be so certain. Maybe I never would.

Back in East Lansing, walking beside the Red Cedar River pushing against its banks, all I knew was that spring had come, how the cool air smelled of pine trees, and how much I liked hearing Bogart's line and the reckless, ironic, hip laughter bursting from that coed's mouth.

Ray

At the memorial service in Atlanta, someone I didn't know recited Ray's accomplishments—the James Baldwin Prize for his first novel, *Appalachee Red* (1978), followed by two more novels, a memoir, and two novellas in a single volume, with all five books appearing within just over a dozen years. Other people spoke of his humble beginnings, amiability, close ties to family, military service to his country. Someone else said, professorially, that Raymond Andrews possessed an almost encyclopedic knowledge of professional baseball and football facts and at that I almost laughed. Not because it wasn't true but because it was—*in spades*—and the appended unintended double entendre that popped in my head, and might have been shocking to some, surely would have made Ray laugh. The tone in the auditorium where we sat, however, was starting to lean toward the somber—moreover we were in a serious place, a library—so a burst of laughter right then, from a white man, a stranger to all but a few, would have played badly. Also, I could feel the temperature in the room rising, for a good many folks had come out for this service, this tribute to a Georgia son who had done well—in many ways very well—but whose near anonymity as a writer on a wider stage was and is, ironically, a famous American tale.

When my turn came to speak, I found myself telling his relatives and friends the following story:

In the spring of our freshman year at Michigan State University, Ray and I boarded a Greyhound bus for Chicago, for a high and mighty weekend in a high and mighty city. We had our return tickets but almost no money—maybe enough for a couple of burgers—and we weren't sure where we'd stay. Ray said no sweat. His older brother Benny would take care of us. We could sleep on Benny's floor as a last resort, or on the floor at one of his girlfriends' places—Benny had girlfriends *all over* Chicago, Ray said. We would be okay. The main thing to remember was: we were going to the Art Students' Ball. Artists, girls. Bohemians. Anything could happen, he said.

This was 1957. Ike was President.

In Chicago, Benny told us we would need costumes, saying, "You didn't know that?"

"Costumes?" Ray said.

"Like Halloween, man, only fancier. Threads of a high creative order."

Ray said, "I guess we forgot about fancy creative threads."

So Benny delivered us to one of his girlfriends who worked in a costume shop. She had only two costumes left: cave man leopard skins, orange-bright with black spots, the totalities of which were just enough to cover our lower loins, a side of ribs, and a small narrow strip over one shoulder.

Ray said, "Fancy." He said, "Man, we'd be practically naked and it's *cold* outside."

We all turned to a large window, beyond which the gray Chicago sky promised rain.

"How would it be," Ray finally suggested, "if we wore these skins *on top* our regular clothes?"

Benny and his girlfriend—both of whom were graduating from the Art Institute, the ball's sponsor—said no, that wouldn't be authentic, wouldn't be getting into the spirit of things. We didn't want to look like a couple of rubes, did we?

"Could we," Ray asked after a moment, "wear our shoes?"

"Well," they said, "maybe no one would notice."

So Ray and I went to the ball, and to several parties beforehand, clad in our cave man outfits *dans* shoes but *sans* socks. We checked out God knew how many attractive girls all got up in exotic costumes, including a panther and a calico cat we especially had our eyes on and whose eyes seemed to be on us. We told them we had journeyed all the way from Michigan State, the land of the Spartans. And when they picked up their tails and crept away—to curry their fur, they said, promising to return—we said to ourselves, "Oh man, this is *it*. How can we fail?"

Sometime early Sunday morning, however, the ball over, the panther and the calico cat gone to wherever such beautiful sleek creatures go for the night, Ray and I sat cold and hungover on the wrong train—one heading not to Benny's floor but north toward Milwaukee, a direction in which we knew no one and no one knew us—two freshman from East Lansing in faux leopard skins, goosebumps, and penny loafers.

"We should have looked for some cave women," Ray said.

RAY WAS TWENTY-THREE THAT YEAR; I was nineteen. He had served four years in the Air Force and been to Korea, been to a lot of places, whereas the few times I had been out of Michigan I was in the company of my parents or a priest. I had been an altar boy; Ray had visited houses of ill repute. ("You know what those are, son?") He was born in rural Georgia, the fourth of ten children; his father was a sharecropper, his mother believed in education. At fifteen, on his first journey more than five miles from home, Ray moved to Atlanta—about an hour away—where, living in the YMCA and shepherded by his oldest brother Harvey who also lived there, he worked a bunch of crummy jobs during the day, he said, and went to Washington High School at night.

"Like crummy how?" I said. "Be clear."

"Like menial crummy."

"Like what the organized would call entry level?"

"That's right. Back-door-to-the-fry-house-kitchen-to-wash-dishes level."

(Lest the reader think Ray's use of *crummy* in this 1957 dialogue characterizes entire his nearly three-year stay in the capital city, a memoir called *Once Upon a Time in Atlanta*, published posthumously in 1998 as a single issue of *The Chattahoochee Review*, shows him confessing to many delights among the hard Dickensian lessons and chores he experienced during that late-teen prelude to joining the Air Force.)

At MSU, Ray and I lived in Butterfield Hall, at first a few doors down from each other. Before we roomed together, I briefly put up with someone called Pendergast, and he drew someone not unlike Pendergast—living arrangements that the university had in place before any of us arrived on campus. My Pendergast was a banker's son from western New York whose plan in life was to go home to Batavia after his four years at MSU and marry Penny and work in his father's bank, eventually taking it over. Meanwhile, he could usually be found stretched out fully dressed on his bed, ankles crossed, smoking and talking with his two high-school friends who had also enrolled at MSU, remembering the famous things they had done growing up in Batavia.

I can see Ray stopping by, leaning in the doorway to catch some of this action. Soon sated, he would nod respectfully toward Pendergast, then at me, and say, "Cool. Very cool."

Between remembering famous things they had done, the two friends, sitting on either side of Pendergast's bed, would implore him to tell them *why* they were in East Lansing, Michigan.

It was, they said, totally nowhere. Pendergast would take long thoughtful pulls on his cigarette and slowly blow rings of smoke at the ceiling. Everyone waited for the last ring to dissipate and then for Pendergast to say, wearily,

"I'm exhausted."

"He says he's exhausted."

"We're all exhausted."

"Exhausted in nowhere."

"We have a problem."

"Pendergast, we have a problem."

I avoided most of this Beckett-lite bitching by studying in the library or by hanging out with Ray, who was my sports friend, or with Dave Kelly, the future poet and my closest literary friend. I also got a job refereeing intramural basketball games after dropping out of trying to make the school team. My interests were changing. I'd fallen in with some serious readers who met—very informally, almost as if by accident, and very coolly—to drink black coffee and spontaneously take up talking about *Billy Budd,* Knut Hamsun, *Native Son*, Keats, Gide. (This loose and independent set of readers would come to include, besides Dave, the future writers J. D. Reed, Tom McGuane, and Jim Harrison.) I had declared a journalism major, like Kelly, but fiction and poetry, the essays of Henry Miller, histories like Edmund Wilson's *To the Finland Station*—these were where the drama was, the passion.

When Pendergast and his Estragon and Vladimir managed to find digs for three, Ray and I became roommates. Our friendship was fueled largely by debating who the great athletes were—and which the great athletic contests—followed closely by identifying the popular singers and actors and movies of importance. Power, grace, and those indefinable facets that allowed one jewel to shine brighter than so many others were our themes. We went round and round, of course, trying to nail

down the indefinable. We also took pleasure in razzing each
other about our heroes and the professional teams we favored,
although I came to notice—and was more and more mindful—
that hard shots at Mickey Mantle could render Ray moodily
silent if the Mick had had a notably bad day. The Yankee blond
bomber ranked as high as a mortal could rank in Ray's eyes.
Ava Gardner and Frank Sinatra shared the Mick's elevation, up
where the air was intoxicating and pure and so sweet it could
cause a honeyed glow in those lucky and fit enough to catch a
whiff of it.

Closer to earth, Ray and I cheered on MSU's football team
and its affable, leprechaunish coach Duffy Daugherty. Duffy was
national Coach of the Year in 1955 for directing the Spartans
to a 9-1 won-lost record, including a dramatic 17-14 victory
over UCLA in the Rose Bowl via a 41-yard field goal by Dave
Kaiser with seven seconds left to play. (This game and season
had a major influence in Ray's decision to enroll at MSU.) The
next fall Duffy's team was 7-2, losing by one touchdown to
Illinois and by one point to Minnesota; and in 1957 the Spartans
were 8-1, their single loss another one-touchdown squeaker.
So autumn was a good time to be in East Lansing, totally nowhere
as it was to some and officially dry as it was to everyone else,
including Ray, who was accustomed to camaraderie around a
few cold brews now and then.

Just beyond the city limits, to the east, lay a popular watering
hole for students of legal drinking age or with fake IDs. Ray
belonged to the MSU Vets Club, whose logo was a drake wearing
a truss, and once a week, usually Friday afternoons, he joined
his fellow ruptured ducks at the Coral Gables to TGIF. Sometimes
he brought back to campus a pint of cheap rye whiskey that we
were very careful not to get caught with, the penalty for which
was immediate banishment from school, no discussion. Often

I had a date on Friday nights, and Ray, if he had a bottle, would walk the campus shadows sipping from it alone.

I never knew Ray to go out with a coed—or any woman—at MSU. When I offered to fix him up with a blind date, he'd hem and haw, studying his shoes, and finally allow, "Okay, describe her. But don't tell me she has pretty hair or a really nice personality. You know what girls with pretty hair or really nice personalities have? Not much else." Usually I only had a description to pass on that had been supplied by my date, and that was never good enough. There was, however, one coed he said he'd like to date: her name was Mary Ann and, by his account, she was very attractive and smart—"Italian," he'd nod approvingly—but alas, shrugging his shoulders, he'd say she was way beyond his reach. What that meant, exactly, he never said, but he let me believe it basically had to do with not having real money to spend. I don't recall ever seeing Mary Ann, only walking with Ray past her dorm on those Friday nights I didn't have a date and keeping him company with his bottle of rye.

Almost from the first time we met I thought Ray's ancestry might have included a Black-white relationship, and when I met Benny in Chicago there was little doubt. But if Ray—who could—wanted to pass for white in East Lansing or simply chose not to give the subject his time, that was fine with me. At one point—after Chicago—I thought to tell Ray I had played baseball in Flint with and against guys who were Black, red, and various hues of white, but what mattered was how well they threw, caught, and hit the ball; then I thought it was not my place to start that conversation.

SOONER OR LATER, IN REMEMBERING Ray, I think about three newsworthy events that took place in that fall of 1957, two of them twin-related, and the third occurring ten days later as if to create a kind of eerily humming Greek chorus to bedevil the nation and to underline, with thudding irony, the first pair. I refer to the "Little Rock Nine" integrating an Arkansas high school on 23 September and President Eisenhower's having to send Federal troops down there—the first time for such action since Reconstruction—to quell the gathering mob. Then, on 4 October, the Russians launched *Sputnik I*, the first earth-orbiting satellite, turning up by several notches America's feelings of insecurity on the global stage.

In this context of fear—same time period—I also think about the only Korea story Ray told me more than once. Its telling usually came when I kept him company on those Friday night walks around campus, the rye loosening him up a bit. The supply plane that brought the troops their new movie every week couldn't deliver during one stretch, so Ray and his fellow film-goers had to hunker down with what they'd already seen, *High Noon*, starring Gary Cooper as the aging, principled sheriff outnumbered by bad guys. Ray said he watched it the nineteen consecutive nights it was shown and each night found himself trying to find something in the story—some detail—he hadn't seen before.

"I always could," he said, "because Coop was *that* good."

"At what?" I always said.

"At what? At keeping me interested in how a man can get from one place to the next—without getting himself killed."

AT THE END OF THAT fall 1957 term, Ray dropped out of sight—my sight, anyway—and would not reappear for twenty-eight years. In late August 1985, when I was living in Des Moines, Iowa, teaching at Drake University, he surfaced: via a note addressed to "Mister Gary Gildner" from "Just Plain Curious / Raymond Andrews," stating that he had had a roommate with my name at Michigan State University in 1957. "But if you are not the same person please disregard this infringement."

I wrote to Ray immediately, and our letters shot back and forth in the following months to fill in the years. A lack of funds—compounded by a low grade-point average—prevented Ray from enrolling for the winter 1958 quarter. He ended up in New York City, where he lived "off and on for the next 26 years." He felt guilty, he said, about not answering the letter I wrote from Butterfield wondering where the hell he was and what he was up to.

On 24 September 1985, Ray starts his third letter to me, saying "Don't get alarmed and feel that you are going to be stuck with lettering. . . . It's just that after nearly thirty years I don't want to lose touch." He goes on to say, "I always wanted to write poetry," jokes about trying to write "a best-selling poem" and instead producing—"being the wordy person I am"—the novel *Appalachee Red.* Eventually he gets around to what hits me as the heart of this letter, confessing: "Coming back at you like this after nearly 30 years I feel I owe you, a former roomie, an explanation (not an apology) of sorts." His explanation *of sorts* (my *Merriam-Webster's* defines "of sorts" as "of an inconsequential or mediocre quality") is difficult and awkward for him but hardly irrelevant. He continues,

> I never knew who at MSU (and there were a few) knew
> me to be black. Before MSU every place I'd gone I made
> the announcement upon arrival as to who I was only
> to find out that the people I usually gravitated to didn't
> much care one way or the other once getting to know
> one another. So that became my philosophy . . . and
> still is . . . like or dislike me for having read PP [*Peyton
> Place*, a popular 1956 novel by Grace Metalious built
> around guilt, hypocrisy, and bales of baleful sex] or
> being a Yankee fan but not for something I have no

control over. And I've done the same for all Tiger and Lions fans.

This last sentence, especially, eloquent in its way, is clearly an appeal to only one fan of Detroit's professional baseball and football teams and to the golden rule. His next sentence shifts immediately from the rocky, ambiguous ground of "philosophy" to the groomed and ruler-straight diamond of baseball, where we could both "know one another." He says—I can almost hear him exhaling in relief—"Speaking of the Yankees, to me they have never been the same since 1964 . . ."

Not quite two years later, in early March, we saw each other in person in Athens, Georgia, at a celebration of *The Georgia Review*'s fortieth anniversary, and Ray again brought up owing me an explanation. We were taking a quiet walk on the grounds around the house that he and Benny had built just outside of town. I pretty much knew where he was headed. I said he didn't owe me anything, that he had explained all he needed to explain—and beautifully—in his novels. Furthermore, I said, my policy over the years hadn't changed: I still treated all Yankees fans the same, no matter how ugly they might be. After a beat, he laughed. Then, picking up on the locker-room banter we had practiced back in Butterfield, he said, "Explain to me again, if you would, about that all-parochial basketball team you got named to in high school. Was that, like, a team of the most limited and narrow-minded?"

"I will be more than happy to explain," I said. "But first, can you help me understand how a professional as potentially cute as Ava Gardner could act like a perfect lump on a log with lips?"

"Cute? That's evil. That shows an absence of real religion in your life."

"On the other hand, a truly stunning woman like Marilyn Monroe—"

"She sure stunned DiMaggio."

We were okay. We knew all what we were talking about without talking about all of it.

RAY WAS A NATURAL TALKER, his delivery honed in a country tradition seasoned with sneaky pokes of dry wit. Once he got warmed up it was hard to be anything but a good audience that couldn't help but let loose claps of appreciation when he hit notes of high lyrical quality—and like any performer, he enjoyed receiving those rewards. He could go on and on about the Mick and Ava and Ol' Blue Eyes as if he knew them personally. Ray moved most at ease, showing his true narrative gifts, when filling an hour at dinner by fleshing out the foibles of those who would strut and bark with little between their ears. But he also had sport with his own imperfections and inclinations—his near-nonexistent cotton-picking abilities as a boy in Georgia, or his life-long strategies for avoiding almost any kind of confrontation, preferring to go down in the record books as a lover, not a brawler.

In carrying on as he did, sliding into position as omniscient reporter hovering over a gathering of folks rich and poor, foolish and wise and prideful, he may well have been practicing, consciously or not, the way he would later construct his by-and-for-the-ear sentences that gave a particular talky, old-time tone and body to his fiction and memoirs. He didn't speak slowly, didn't drawl or ham, that's for sure, but like certain nuns I'd had in grade school he could give a close impression of doing so, of unduly stretching time itself like the skinniest ply of spider web, drawing you in, the words themselves uncannily springing forth as if he'd had to journey miles down a dirt road under a hot sun to fetch them—and only now, as he allowed himself a moment of rest here in the shade with his good friends, could he let these precious words flow free like cool—or icy cold—murmuring water.

Here, from *Appalachee Red,* is Poor Boy Jackson kneeling beside the bed of his young teenage daughter Baby Sweet, telling her via one long circling Andrews sentence that she is in deep troubled water there in Hard Labor Hole for having danced her provocative "Fuzz Shake" where the white peach farmer Mist' Ed, for whom Poor Boy works, could see it and get ideas:

> Without a word of her own she listened to her daddy talking in this rediscovered voice of his, mostly about how just the day before he had told her to stop her sinful ways, especially in front of the white folks, and now the merciful and just Good Lord was seeing fit to punish her for her evildoing and there was nothing in the world he, her daddy who had warned her, could do about the Lord's punishment upon her soul except to pray—which she should start doing herself and right that minute—without losing his job and there were still too many mouths left in the house there to be fed for him, the father, to allow such a thing to come to pass.

Ray came from people who quickened to stories, *listened* to them. He told me, in Athens, that he had thought about being a writer for a long time, even before he was fully aware of it himself. At MSU, whether telling a tale to a tableful in the dorm dining room—Ma Brody's—or intimately in our room, smoking a Lucky, he never mentioned the notion of putting any of these yarns and anecdotes down on paper. And when Dave Kelly came by the room and he and I got to talking about Fitzgerald or Hemingway and the pursuit, craft, and passion of writing, Ray fell silent. He had nothing to say.

Those decades later he would confess to me in a letter that writers to him then were the likes of Luke Short and Zane Grey and Harold Robbins; the latter's novel *Dream Merchants* Ray thought "a classic," and by classic he meant superior, masterly. In that same letter, he recalls that when he told me of spending the summer becoming "intellectualized" by reading *Peyton Place,* I had "cut the whole season short by telling me that PP was a piece of shit. It being a best-seller too! This I *couldn't* understand. So right away I told you that Mickey Mantle could *kick* Al Kaline's ass!" The Milwaukee Braves would defeat his beloved New York Yankees in the World Series that fall of 1957, four games to three—the great Mick was unable to save them—but my hoots in that quarter could not make him feel any gloomier. Who *were* these writers that Gildner and Kelly admired so much at the same time they were dismissing such big successes as Erle Stanley Gardner and Ellery Queen?

WHAT RAY WAS UP TO after dropping out of MSU was making a living—reservations agent for KLM Airlines, librarian for Pix Photographers, mailroom clerk, messenger, telephone operator, bookkeeper—and writing. At one point, in 1966, he sold to *Sports Illustrated,* for $250, a charming shades-of-Mark-Twain account of the first football game played in rural Plainview, Georgia ("pop. 222"), where he grew up. He and brother Benny, ages twelve and sixteen, respectively, are the opposing major-domo quarterbacks in this got-up kid-zany contest played in a cow pasture with a ragged tennis ball, shouting out the names of cars instead of using numbers when calling signals ("because most of the fellows weren't too familiar with figures"). Each side featured thirteen players—"blocking, tackling, holding, clipping, biting and gouging"—to accommodate the twenty-six boys wanting to play. "My next work"—his first novel, *Appalachee Red*—"sold twelve years later so that $250 had to stretch a ways."

The year 1966 was lively and important for Ray: his SI article appeared in the 7 November issue; he married Adelheid Wenger, an airlines sales agent, three days after Christmas; and he quit his job at KLM to have more time for writing. In a 1985 letter he says, "I got married to a young lady from Switzerland, Heidi, of course, and for the next thirteen years we were to live back and forth between there and here. She was, is, an opera singer and the clashing of careers (plus her needing to live and work in Europe and me here) brought an end to the marriage in 1980. No children. Just two cats, which she won in the settlement." Here is a clutch of seventy words blending the Horatio Alger story, a Hollywood movie plot (including the classic "clashing of careers" cliché), and a soft, furry ending that suggests everything is okay.

Such a neat mixed-bag précis makes me smile, watching the writer practicing his craft. I wish I could say this to him. I had my chance in Athens, but my ugly Yankees-fans crack got out first. Mixed, medley, mélange, pastiche, composite, assortment: all these cousins—blood kin, friends, enemies, and passersby alike—were *always* in Ray's house, over his shoulder making mischief, making love, just plain carrying on as he was shaping up stories influenced by them, by rags, riches, the movies, the good and the bad. *Lord, Lord*—as Ray would so often exclaim.

There is no doubt that Ray paid some weighty dues in getting from those cotton fields in Plainview to New York City and the life of a writer. Nor is there any doubt that he had no interest in choosing up sides in any old racial or political fights; he said this—and in his books demonstrates it—often enough. He was interested in story, in telling a good one, the best one he could. If that story insisted on handing out warts all around, regardless of race, creed, etc., so much the better. Indeed, the warts helped clear a path among the clichés he couldn't avoid: those weeds and weevils of speech gripping his land and his hand. Ray Andrews's characters are Black, white, and, one way or another, in between. Is one group fated to be more pure, less pure, more prone to error than any other? Lord, have mercy. Was Raymond Andrews, the grandson of Mister Jim, a white man, ever prone to intellectualizing such a briary theme? Lord, show me the way.

> Lonzo knew his white customers well, how they always appeared at his place acting in that apologetic way of theirs that they reserved for such situations, ever with an excuse for how it came about that they had to come to him—meaning, buying liquor, always, in the middle of the night over in Dark Town from a nigger. No, they could never just buy their liquor and leave it at that; they always felt some explanation was due—an old friend had just popped into town, some special occasion was being celebrated, or anything else but the cold fact that they just wanted, or needed, a drink and nothing more. Lonzo had come to call all of this excusing, apologizing, and such the "Cracker Shuffle." And, oh, yes, the joke. They never felt they would be permitted to leave without telling a little joke, the "nigger-pacifier," as they *knew* from the cradle that nobody liked to laugh more than a nigger and a white man telling a joke would—they had never seen or heard of it to fail—put the nigger on the verge of rupturing himself from laughing . . . or straining to laugh . . . to make him forget his child-like problems . . . and the fact that they themselves had just crawled over the Wall to buy nigger's liquor. Anyhow, Lonzo didn't care what excuses they gave or how many jokes they told, just so long as they paid for what they bought. (from *Appalachee Red*)

During this signal, exciting period in Ray's life when many weeks he could sit down seven straight days to be a writer, he was also catching up on his reading. "It was only after leaving MSU that I started to read *real* writers. That's when I got into Faulkner and became convinced he [was] America's best writer . . . though I feel *Gatsby* is America's best *written* book. Not a single word lost. *Peyton Place*? It needs more time."

ON 7 MARCH 1987, IN Athens, as part of its fortieth anniversary celebration, *The Georgia Review* hosted an evening of readings by Mary Hood, Lee K. Abbott, and me because our stories had won for it the 1986 National Magazine Award in Fiction. Stanley Lindberg, the *Review*'s editor, asked Ray to introduce me. I was the first reader on the program and first readers at such notable events, among friends they want to be good for, will sometimes admit to being nervous. I don't think I was nervous because of all that, but my internal machinery *was* made to move rapidly in a variety of directions by Ray's introduction. He himself seemed calm—and why not? This was his town. He had been living here, ate pizza and drank beer here, and was known to take great pleasure in trading stories around tables of friends here. At the podium he went back to Michigan State and told about our rooming together in Butterfield and arguing sports and about how he wanted to be a writer but had no idea—not really—who these people F. Scott Fitzgerald and Papa Hemingway *were* that I talked about with my other friends, and therefore he kept his mouth shut and started to read and wanted to thank me.

It was—not to put too fine a point on it—a once-in-a-lifetime introduction, and I felt it. I feel it now. I feel it especially now having read all his books and knowing so much of his story and how he worked it and reworked it, mixing and matching: here playing to his audience, going all the way to give the dressers what they dressed up for, the spenders what they peeled off their greenbacks for; and there staying cool, poised, waiting for his pitch, like the Mick.

In Ray's first three novels—*Appalachee Red* (1978), *Rosiebelle Lee Wildcat Tennessee* (1980), and *Baby Sweet's*

(1983)—a trilogy I still cannot understand how I completely missed seeing as the books came out!—he borrows materials from the world he knew well, as serious writers will: the cotton fields of Plainview (he spells it Plain View), the towns of Madison and Apalachee (he adds an extra *p*), the Oconee River and Hard Labor Creek (he makes it Hard Labor Hole)—all can be found, pretty much where they are in Ray's books, on a Georgia map. In *Appalachee Red* the White House that Little Bit gets her rich white employer-lover to build for her—if she's going to gain anything from sharing his bed while her Black husband, Big Man Thompson, rages in prison—is inspired by the house, painted white, that Mister Jim built for Ray's grandmother. Both grandparents, by the way, are waved to fondly in *Rosiebelle Lee Wildcat Tennessee* ("This was My Grandmother, Name and All, Hope You Enjoy it," he wrote in my copy) and dialed up direct in the memoir *The Last Radio Baby* (1990). And in this house built for Little Bit that eventually becomes a casino run by Little Bit's and the white man's red baby grown big and fearsome, there is a radio turned only to boxing matches and baseball games, as was the radio in the home of Ray's youth, whenever he had any say in the matter. And then he got to say all of it, the whole story out of Plain View, Georgia, seasoned with some shavings from, but not limited to, *Peyton Place, High Noon,* and *The Great Gatsby;* from those rye-toned strolls in the shadows past the dorm of unobtainable Mary Ann; and from the haints. All stirred up over a low flame.

Haint is a word Ray uses in all of his books. My favorite instance occurs in *The Last Radio Baby*, where he tells how his Aunt Marie

> believed in ghosts, or "haints," and knew all of the haint hangouts in Plainview. It was through Aunt Marie that I found out haints weren't good "mudders," hating to haint when it was raining. There was another funny

thing about haints—regardless of a person's color alive, he or she returned as a "white" haint. I never heard of anyone who saw a "colored" haint. Death bleached.

My *Merriam-Webster's* doesn't have the word, though *hailstorm* and *hair*—between which it could snuggle—do provide a promising enough neighborhood. My older *Standard College Dictionary* (1963), from Funk & Wagnalls, does have *hain't*— defined as "(hānt) Illit. & Dial. 1. Have not. 2. Has not." Which is pretty close in an odd, pale, poetic kind of way. This poetic proximity is precisely why I slip mention of the word into my essay to present Ray: because it functions, I believe, as a kind of signal, hint, perhaps even—to get fancy and risk clever punning—an objective correlative: an impersonal means of communicating feeling. Consider, in this light, the newspaper stories that follow.

In 1990 I published *The Warsaw Sparks*, a memoir about living in Communist Poland for fourteen months, teaching American literature at the University of Warsaw and coaching a Polish baseball team. The book moved Ray to send me clippings from the *New York Times* about Polish life before, during, and after Communism. There was the countess who went from a childhood in Warsaw's royal estate, Wilanów, to the three-year nightmare of a Soviet labor camp, chopping wood; released, she and her two sisters earned what they could at the most menial of work and ate in soup kitchens. There was the poet and playwright Agnieszka Osiecka remembering her father, who railed against the Communists but also against the Catholic church, patriots, frugality, dullness—in short, against what most people subscribed to—borrowing money to buy his family expensive raspberries in January and, in exceptionally good moods, sitting down at a beat-up piano to play "The Man I Love" for this lucky daughter. There was Janusz Glowacki, living in New York almost a decade: he had fled a government that banned his novel about the birth of Solidarity, *Give Us This Day,* and he now debated whether to return. Poland was still his country, but following the Soviet collapse he lamented, "Polish National TV airs Roman Catholic services interlaced with episodes of *Miami Vice,*" and he would not be surprised to see the same people who once banned his play *Hunting Cockroaches* for being anti-Communist now stopping it for being anti-capitalist. "Maybe I belong nowhere," he said, "and I am simply dangling somewhere in the middle."

Such stories about people from high, low, and in-between stations, their lives romantic, threatened, rescued by panache, or stalled in irony, had an obvious appeal to Ray. "I hope you like this," he'd pen on a clipping. "I did."

And here, by the way, was another story he took to: about our fellow MSU student J. D. Reed who—unlike the rest of us serious readers drinking black coffee and mulling Melville pondering *Moby-Dick*—had money enough to splurge on a big new luxury station wagon—and did—because, as he roared mockingly more than once, "It is so obscene!" After MSU, J. D. published a collection of poems that received good notices, time passed, and when last heard from he was reviewing books for *People*—including *The Last Radio Baby.* He called it "a cross between *Roots* and *A Prairie Home Companion.*" Back at MSU Ray would have been far too shy to even pull up a chair and drink anything with this affluent young literary lion cub moving in high ironic gear; but Ray was not too unconfident to take on until death parted them the cousins, the demons, the haints, and any who fell into his extended colorful view and wouldn't leave him alone—not so much because they wanted to make something big of themselves but because he wanted to make something interesting of them.

REREADING OUR CORRESPONDENCE (RAY'S LETTERS typed on a good bond—often both sides; mine carbon copies on onionskin, typed with a manual Royal), I sometimes feel myself smiling at how many people nowadays would view these pieces of paper as downright quaint. A fair number of the words and sentiments expressed on them might be viewed as old-fashioned too, perhaps even odd—"inspired," for example, leaps out like a beloved arthritic dog you were sure had curled into his personal heap for keeps ages ago, but now is rejuvenated, wanting to play. Ray and I are talking about what writers typically talk about between and among themselves: writing and books, including our own, and doing what we can to get by, help out. At times we sound almost giddy—and transported back to 1957 swagger. Naturally we are still interested in sports and women and a convivial brew; and we are not above an occasional dip with Narcissus. There is an attempt in the letters, I reckon, to right something—call it a friendship—that got thrown off course by the vagaries we are all given a share of as we put one foot in front of the other; or an attempt to brighten something—call it a good story—whose many parts we might have traded back and forth for a long time. But something relentless, indifferent, and far more inspired than either of us could ever want to be stepped in and put a stop to our Shake 'n Bake strut.

A MONTH AFTER THE RELEASE OF the twinned novellas *Jesse and Jesus* and *Cousin Claire* (1991), Ray's last work of fiction, Benny found Ray's body in the back yard of their Athens home. Benny had just arrived from New York to spend Thanksgiving. They were close, these two brothers, close enough for Benny to illustrate Ray's books—all of them—with lean-lined, ghost-glossed drawings that often want to dance, saunter, or fall, full of themselves, off the paper that Ray, I can imagine, is still fussily writing on in his lean block lettering. Sometimes Benny's black-

and-white figures are hangdog lonesome, sitting on the edge of a big, wide bed, and sometimes they stand before a tombstone in postures shaped by years that have eked out small relief.

Ray shot himself. He was ill, the note he left behind said— "very seriously," Benny told me—and was choosing this way rather than descend into lingering, hanging on by his finger-nails and becoming a burden.

Six months later, Raymond Andrews would be posthumously given the American Book Award for *Jessie and Jesus* and *Cousin Claire,* a darkly comedic work contrasting two strong African American women—lusty Jesse and quiet Claire—and how they go about getting what they want. The American Book Award is given by the Before Columbus Foundation "to respect and honor excellence in American literature without restriction or bias with regard to race, sex, creed, cultural origin, size of press or ad budget, or even genre," according to a Peachtree Publishing news release. Previous recipients included Toni Morrison, Louise Erdrich, John Edgar Wideman, and Allen Ginsberg. Ray would have been thrilled and deeply moved, I'm sure. Moreover, he would have had no trouble handling an invitation—had one come to pass—to socialize with this distinguished and powerful set of winners.

Let's imagine such an invitation materialized, followed— bingo-bango—by an invitation to socialize—same day, same time—with a somewhat different set. Now let's mix and match, just for fun; let's say that second invitation is to join the celebration in the Yankees clubhouse right after they take the seventh game of the World Series against the Dodgers, capping a season in which the Mick wins the rare Triple Crown (best batting average, most home runs, most runs batted in) *and* is named the American League's Most Valuable Player—all of which is true regarding Mantle and the Yankees in the autumn of 1956, when my future roommate became a Spartan. But the question isn't really about which invitation Ray would accept—it's about some long-shot odds: that first invitation is merely possible, whereas the second is too dear to trust to chance—and so we can only dream it.

Ray Andrews wanted to jump and shout. His stories—those calls and responses and bawdy, moaning organ tropes—celebrate, deep down, what he once told me back in Butterfield he was no good at: singing and dancing. This might well have been a joke with a serious point that I was too slow to get right away; and if he *was* trying to tell me something, I didn't hear it until I started reading those first three novels—that trilogy—he proudly sent me. Oh yes, indeed, Ray wanted to jump and shout, get sweaty, get down and dirty, but he didn't want to get caught being clumsy or false—which is one reason he hung with such smooth actors as Mickey Mantle and Frank Sinatra. Downriver, on yonder bank, he also hung with James Brown and the Robinsons—Jackie and Sugar Ray—among others; but while we were roommates Ray was looking into and testing the waters on our bank, too—which might be called the *Everyday Bank*—as, now and then, he had before. The result was the work, flowing impure, pure, and simple. And, as far as I can tell, nobody in Ray's world who is old enough to want a taste of the dangerous fruits growing along the shores is allowed to slide on by without paying a heavy penny. Not even the comic Big Apple, the Black who insists he's a "brown-skinned Jew," gets away with his duplicity: he survives by his wits well enough, but those wits have also twisted round and round a far, far bend. Amen.

AFTER THE FORMAL PART OF the memorial service in the Atlanta-Fulton Public Library that Saturday in early February 1992, some of us moved to Rocky's Brick Oven on Peachtree Street where we ate and drank under the oaks in the yard and remembered things about Ray—little things mainly—that made us feel closer to him and to ourselves, and better. Several people came up and thanked me for that leopard skins story. It made them laugh, they said. We must have had *some* time, they said. Yes, I said, we sure did. I did not add—because I did not have the words then—but from at least the moment I held that spotted cloth against my chest, I have been thinking about those chance moments in life when something as fake as a cave man outfit can say something true (or true at a slant) about the difficulties and burdens of getting from here to there—or, in Ray's case and in mine, from there to here.

Where the Dog Is Buried

In Prague, when Lizzie and I asked an official about taking the train to Prešov, she said, "I do not advise it. It is a filthy method. The only way to Slovakia, if one must go there, is by plane." She made a face like she'd just lost a filling.

I exchanged dollars for crowns. On the hundred-crown note a man and woman stood side by side, he wearing welder's gear, his shirt open, she in overalls, a babushka, a sheaf of wheat under her arm. In the background, industrial chimneys poured smoke into the sky. The pair gazed straight ahead, workers sharing the load. They might have been drawn by Norman Rockwell, except there was no humor, no irony, no surprise in their faces or anywhere else . . .unless you counted a kind of halo that hovered over their heads, constructed from a gear wheel, wheat berries, and coils of steel. Once upon a time they were the new saints, but that fall of 1992, the Velvet Divorce looming, who knew what they were; this bank note was pre-revolution (pre-1989) and would soon be replaced.

Prešov lay ten hours to the east, almost in Ukraine. Our compartment was clean and comfortable, and we saw much more than we could have from a plane: kids beating dust from rugs, geese in single file following an old woman across a field, tidy apple orchards whose cidery scent wafted our way. In small towns we passed through, the stationmasters stood at attention in their doorways, hats on, shoulders back, and saluted. We went between autumn hills, through tunnels into piney corridors, past streams, beside a lake that reflected our waving arms. I was fifty-four, Lizzie thirty-eight—the only time, she pointed out, when my age would match the year of her birth and vice versa. I thought about chance and how I was now a grandfather traveling to Slovakia and planning to walk in the Polish village that my grandfather, then a teenager, had walked away from, carrying his loaf of bread. I thought about how intently he gazed into the northern Michigan sky those summers he sat in his apple orchard while I, a boy in a tree, watched him and wondered, as I wondered on the train, what he was looking for.

Outside Prešov we were delivered to a huge housing estate called Sečov, named—we learned later—for a brook that the development had destroyed. We also learned that our street, Dumbierska, meant something like *ginger*, that the road connecting us to Prešov was Sibirska—meaning "Siberia"—and that the 38 bus would carry us back and forth for two crowns. But the first time we went to Sečov was in Igor's Škoda, at night, and laughing, he said he was trying not to get lost.

After the lush, dreamy countryside we'd seen all day, Sečov was sobering. Prefab high-rises surrounded us. I tried to count them once, weeks later, and lost interest. They all looked alike, cement-colored, nine stories—dormitories plunked down in a raw, treeless setting. Ours was new, Igor told us: "You will be the first occupants of your flat!"

An elevator not much larger than a phone booth—basically a platform in a shaft—took us up six floors. You could touch the building's skeleton as you rose. Igor, squeezed in with us, said in his acquired British accent, "Is it all right then?" He'd asked the same thing about our mailbox down in the entryway. He was my chair at the university, a man who got up on the balls of his feet a lot and showed you the big gap between his front teeth, his eyes bulging. He'd met our train and brought us directly to what he called "the new digs," where he commenced to show us all our keys: building key, mailbox key, flat key, and the remaining six that—he demonstrated— would unlock the bedroom, living room, toilet, bath, kitchen, and a large foyer closet.

"Is it all right then?"

"Everything looks fine." I didn't know what else to say. The important business seemed to be that all the keys worked.

"Fine then." He shook our hands, started to leave, stopped. "Oh, did you bring food? You're not hungry, I hope." We said we were fine. "Fine then. Ah yes, Professor Grmela and his wife will call on you tomorrow with certain details. Cheerio!"

WE TURNED ON THE TV in the living room. Young women paraded in evening gowns, bathing suits: a beauty contest. They all had long, gorgeous legs and exaggerated the swing in their hips as if in parody. They took turns caressing a new Škoda, falling onto new sofas, having their high, shiny cheekbones dusted with powders, modeling furs and leather motorcycle jackets and jewelry; they held up glossy photos of cocktail lounges and swimming pools and airplanes. All these products and pictures were praised by a tux-clad, toothy master of ceremonies. When he paused, a voice off camera sang, in English, "Only you can make my life complete." Almost every Saturday night, we discovered, we could turn on the TV and see a contest like this one.

In the middle of the night we were wakened by a wail from the flat above. It was a man's voice, and his long, melancholy cry seemed to say that no one, no one, could help him. But then we heard a woman's voice—from the same place—and its barklike syllables apparently came to his rescue. In moments the wail trailed into silence. This, too, seemed a regular weekend event.

LOOKING STRAIGHT DOWN FROM OUR living-room window, we could see what appeared to be a gigantic unfinished basement. It seemed long and wide as a soccer field, had partitions for rooms, and was full of water. This had been the start of a neighborhood bunker, but work came to a halt the day the revolution arrived because the builders no longer knew who would pay them and walked off the job. It had sat three years now collecting rain, tossed stones, refuse, and rats.

Almost daily a small boy on a tricycle would appear down there and ram the bunker's outer wall, then back up a few yards, lower his head and, pedaling hard, ram the wall again. He did this over and over until his mother arrived to lead him away. At first we feared for him: feared he would become bored and climb the wall—which was not much taller than he was—and maybe fall into the water. But he never got off his trike that we could see; he had a mission, somewhere to get to, a job to do—and this thing, this stupidity, was in his path. It made him mad, and ramming it was all he could do.

THAT FIRST SUNDAY MORNING, ANITA and Nicole, the daughters of Josef and Anna Grmela, arrived at our door with bread, fruit, tea. "Our parents wish to come at one o'clock and take you to lunch," said one. "They would have called, but you haven't a phone," said the other. Anita and Nicole were eighteen and seventeen, blonde, freckled, cheerful, and curious.

"Are you glad you're here? I mean in Slovakia?" Nicole asked.

"Yes, we are," Lizzie said. "Aren't we, Dr. G.?"

"You call your husband by his title?" said Anita.

"It's a joke," Lizzie said. "I call him that, sometimes, because he's not a doctor."

"Weren't you a little afraid to come?" Nicole asked.

"What should we be afraid of?" Lizzie said.

"People here are afraid," said Anita. "They don't know what will happen after the separation."

"Even our parents are concerned," Nicole said.

"We're Czech, not Slovak," Anita said.

I asked where they lived. Through the window they pointed toward a small mountain in the distance.

"Šariš Castle is up there, or what remains."

"It resembles a cake."

"In fact, eggs were used in the mortar."

"And you live up there, on that mountain?" Lizzie asked.

"No, no," Anita laughed. "Below it. In Development Number Three."

"But there is no egg in the mortar," Nicole said.

"No, it is not a cake, I'm afraid," replied Anita.

AT ONE THEIR PARENTS ARRIVED, Anna vivacious as her daughters, Josef barrel-chested, red-bearded, freckled. They took us on the 38 bus to a hotel in town. Anna said, "I know in the West—especially in America, I think—that people invite you in, not out. Here it seems to be the reverse. But very soon, when things are calmer, you must come to our home." She consulted the menu. "Veal is their best dish. Is that all right?"

Josef said, "I for my part must try to avoid anything with flavor these days." He ordered carrots and soy croutons, and though he wanted coffee, Anna said, "Not today."

"I never contradict my wife," he said. "It's the only rule I faithfully keep."

"He is having an experience," she said.

"Yes, for fifty years my kidneys enjoyed themselves and their work and never complained. Now one of them, according to science, may be proposing a revolution. Very dull politics, believe me."

We liked the Grmelas. Words—conversation—seemed to make them spontaneously happy. Especially out in the open. If they'd pointed to a leafy branch where we all might sit and imitate bird calls, I would not have been surprised. In the halls of the university, later, they would sound more like their colleagues, who did not sing, certainly not foolishly in a tree in the year when Czechoslovakia was splitting apart and everything, at any moment, might topple. But on that first day, strolling cobbled streets almost nine hundred years old, there was nothing more dangerous around us than a Gothic church, the Renaissance town hall, the subtle perfumes of autumn, arches with lions' heads, and look, up there, on that chimney—a stork nest!

At a sweetshop we bought ice-cream cones—*zmrzlina*—and Lizzie pushed out her lips to try the word. "*Shmers*lina!"

"Do you like it as well as American ice cream?" Anna asked.

"Mmm, maybe better. And I *think* it's my first cone since our wedding."

"Since your wedding!" Anna said.

"We've only been married a little more than a year," Lizzie told her.

"You're practically on your honeymoon, then. Josef, we should have a party."

"If you will pardon me, I think honeymoons should be left entirely to the principals involved." He said this while keeping a careful eye on the small dip of vanilla he'd been allowed.

Anna said, "I meant of course a party to honor their anniversary. In my excitement I wasn't clear."

"Perhaps," Josef said. "Anniversaries early in a marriage are a very delicate matter."

"He always talks like this," Anna said to us. Josef made a mild grumble of protest. "I mean when you are having fun, dear Josef."

"I'm now reminded of my duty as a representative of the Philosophical Faculty to explain to our visiting Fulbright professor certain nuances, shall we say, in the academic system here."

"Please, Josef, we are enjoying our ice cream."

"The discussion about the quality of this food, in fact, reminded me of our grading methodology. Are you curious?"

"Shoot."

"Yes, shoot. We have three grades—Excellent, Very Good, and Good."

"No Fail?"

"If a student does not receive one of our three grades, he fails."

"So there are four grades."

"You could say so, but we only count the first three."

"Good must be the average grade, what we call *C* in the States."

"No. The most popular grade is Excellent, followed by Very Good. Almost no one receives Good, which is a disgraceful mark."

"Most of the students are above average?"

"Most are quite average. What I explained is what is done."

"Oh, Josef," Anna said, "look at the sky." He did. "Is it excellent?"

"Clearly."

"Is it complete and independent and pure, would you say?"

"I would say so."

"And beautiful?"

"That too, absolutely."

"Thank you."

ALPHABETS AND MAPS

THE FALL WIND BLEW DOWN all night from the Tatra Mountains, and sometimes we woke before dawn, smelling the pines it had come through, and told our dreams.

"I was studying Polish. Trying to carry the alphabet home across a field. I kept dropping letters in the tall grass."

"I was a girl again, walking along the Mississippi, searching for a little boat I'd lost."

Once, after a dream about my grandfather, I looked at the Polish map. His village, Ostrów, was reachable by bus, but we needed time. We didn't want to rush, and we wanted good weather. I also wanted to be ready, I told Lizzie, not exactly sure what I meant.

Often, those mornings, we went up the street to buy a round loaf of fresh-baked bread. I spoke broken Polish to the old woman, and she replied, laughing. She was always pleased that we preferred her specialty, rye made with potatoes. Most mornings after breakfast I stayed in the flat to write, and Lizzie took the 38 bus to my office, which was quiet and had excellent light from a large window facing north. She could make her pastels, with the radio on, and not disturb anyone. She could also play the office piano, which was in there, Josef suspected, because no one knew where else to put it; the stacked marble tiles, stone planters, broken tables—all these were there for the same reason, he supposed. "Really, you have a large closet," he said, "with one wonderful window." The inner wall had two small openings with removable covers—"not so wonderful"— that looked down into a lecture hall. "Originally," Josef said, "a camera was operated from in here; people were surreptitiously observed." My office was at the top of a stairway from the building's main foyer—a handsome, almost elegant stairway you'd sooner expect in a castle.

One day I went looking for Josef, but he wasn't around. Monika, the department's young, blonde secretary, greeted me as she often did: "Oh, my English! No good!" On the bulletin board I noticed the results of a contest for the best student essay in English. The winner was from nearby Poprad. I looked at his picture—he was wearing a tuxedo—and then read his essay, which was printed underneath. He wrote, "Although the great majority of Slovaks wish to keep the Federation, they will do nothing about it. They will let the nationalist fanatics have their way." I asked Monika. "Have you read this? Is it true?"

"Yes, of course."

"But why is it true?"

She rolled her eyes. "For me, no politics. I like young people—for example this handsome boy in the picture—who I hope will continue to be handsome—and cooking and—how do you call it?—computers. Also psychology!"

Monika's bubbly friend, Mary, a secretary in the geography department, on the floor below, came in. "Mary," I said, "can you help me find a map of Slovakia? None of the stores seems to have one."

"Slovakia? Oh, la-la, I wonder."

"Yes, yes, we can do that," Monika said, taking my hand. "Tomorrow. For now, join with us and enjoy a cigarette, yes?" She patted my hand. Her long nails were pearl colored; Madonna's face was printed everywhere on her blouse. I thanked them, no. Monika let go of my hand to answer the telephone. She spoke rapidly in Slovak, set the phone on her desk, came back and seized my hand again. All this caused Mary to bubble more. "Yes," Monika said, "you must sit." Mary sat in a chair to show me how. They were flirting, we all knew it, and meanwhile the phone lay on the desk.

"Your call." I pointed.

Mary popped up, fired mock-serious-secretarial Slovak into the phone, then laid it down and returned to our little meeting. I had to laugh; they did too, Monika patting my hand, Mary showing me how to sit, the caller, perhaps a friend of theirs, perhaps also laughing, and why not? Who could imagine such silliness under the old system? But what about the young man from Poprad, his essay, his warning against apathy? Oh, him, yes. His English is very good! Very. And how nice he looks in his tuxedo, like on TV. Then Lizzie showed up in her baseball cap and aviator scarf, and Monika said, "Here is your woman!" They greeted each other; the bubbly meeting was now larger. The phone was still on the desk, a tiny, tinny voice escaping, and Monika produced a Czech-English dictionary to find a good word that would help us continue—"Pages and pages! This book is so big!"

JOSEF AND ANNA'S FLAT WAS basically like ours except the furniture was nicer and there were many books and pictures. "We have been here," Josef said, "seventeen years." He laughed, "I won't tell you where we lived before; I can't bear to remember it." Anna served soup made with fresh morels picked from the nearby woods. They gave us the best seats, so we could see the central yard—where grass and trees had been planted, years ago, to soften the near view—and then the woods beyond. The hardwoods were turning red and yellow.

Nicole was not there. She had got up at five that morning to dig carrots in the country for spending money. She would earn a hundred crowns for a full day, Josef said. "A grand sum," Anita smiled, letting us know she didn't think it worth the effort. She had recently returned from a year in Connecticut on a government scholarship—one of only three high-school students in Czechoslovakia to receive such a grant—and now she knew, even more than before, what things were worth. Her sweatshirt said OXFORD; she planned to be an academic like her parents.

Anna brought out a casserole of chicken breasts and paprika and cheese. "Our lunch," she said. "But Josef will have vegetables and rice."

"I have three guardian angels watching everything I eat," he said.

"Nicole is the worst," Anna laughed, "and so sharp-tongued about it. She caught him drinking coffee at the university and practically made a speech."

"Yes, Nicole is my sharpest critic."

"As sharp as any you've had." Anna shook her head.

Josef laughed. "I was thinking recently about those Kennedy books that got me in dutch."

"What happened?" Lizzie asked.

"Typical nonsense," he said. "A boring story. But humorous in a way. I had library duty in those days, in addition to my teaching. Six copies of *Profiles in Courage* arrived—the U.S. Embassy in Prague sent them—and I put them in the library. A young colleague, who was in the Party, saw them and at his monthly meeting stood up and said to the Party chief, a man whose IQ I don't believe could be measured, it was so low—a real, well, a real *dumb* man . . . Anyway, this colleague—"

"Who is still on the faculty," Anna broke in.

"Yes, yes, that's right," Josef said. "Anyway, he said to his chief that copies of a book by the imperialist John Kennedy were in the library, and he wondered if faculty member Grmela was ideologically ripe enough to be responsible . . ."

"Ideologically rigid enough, you mean," Anna corrected.

"What did I say?"

"You said 'ripe.'"

"Oh, well," he laughed, "I must be reaching for something. In any case, this Party boss decided to freeze my salary and take away my specialty course, American literature." He sighed. "But you know, Anna, we all compromised ourselves to one degree or another. No one was untouched."

"He is too generous," she told us. "Even as a student he paid."

"No, no," he protested, "that's too far back; it's ancient history."

"You should tell them."

"I've said enough. I will sound like a crybaby, if I don't already."

Anna said, "When Josef was at the School of Economics in Prague, he got caught listening to Radio Free Europe. They expelled him. Made him work for six years as a clerk before he could enroll again."

"A lucky thing," he sighed. "I would have made a lousy economist—the country would be even worse off than now."

Anita pointed out that the sun had left the yard but was still brilliant in the woods beyond.

"Yes, a walk," Josef declared. "Under the common trees with us!"

Outside, Anna said he should have been a forester. "I will use my next life with great pleasure," he said, "perhaps sampling one of those lookout towers in the American West—pondering such expressions as *pardner* and wearing a ten-gallon hat."

Anita smiled. "My father has been to Pittsburgh."

"Yes," he said, "I was there in '89, during the revolution. But you see the kind of luck I have? Every time I go away, something nice happens," he joked.

"They only let you go, finally," Anna said, "because they knew something bad was about to happen, and they wanted to be on your good side."

"The truth is we do not know why they let me go abroad. My guess is a bureaucratic blunder. By the way," he said to me, "I am suddenly reminded that you are having a bureaucratic experience regarding residence cards. Let me just say—then we can enjoy our walk—that it is not necessary to possess such cards. It is only necessary to apply for them. As long as you make an application you are within the law, even if the process takes forever. All you need is to be strong when matters become absurd."

"We should go to the castle," Anita said. "For some romance."

I walked beside her. "You must have deer in these woods," I said.

"We used to have a lot, but now there are none. The Communists shot one whenever they liked. My girlfriend ate deer tongue so often she got bored with it."

Fog clung to the castle ruins. We climbed a stone stairway, dodged trees growing through walls, and stopped on a grassy plateau in the lee of a leaning turret. "The former cake," I said.

"Yes," Anita smiled, opening her backpack. "But I have real cake, apple cake made from an old Moravian peasant recipe."

I thought of my Polish grandmother and of sitting with my chin on the oilcloth covering her kitchen table, with its waxy, leathery, vinegary smell, and then smelling the fresh coffee cake she brought from the oven, an aroma that changed everything.

Lizzie took pictures of us in the fog, and then we started down a path to Šariš village. We heard a rifle shot. Maybe, I said to Anita, there was one deer left. She said no, it was probably a rabbit. Josef pointed toward a cluster of Roma shanties in the trees. I thought of the fluid earth-colored drawings in a children's book Lizzie brought home in which trees might be animals and animals might be people and people might be trees again, but you had to look close.

EXPRESSION

I WENT TO MEET MY REQUALIFIERS, the former teachers of Russian. Using English, especially in front of their peers, was difficult for them. "We don't want to sound stupid," Xenia said. "After all, we are teachers." I kept praising their efforts and challenging them, and in the way, more or less, that a rusty nut can be unbound with oil and a wrench, they began to loosen up.

Drahomira Dragonova ("Call me Dada, maybe is easier for you") was an exception. She was a professor of philosophy, and married to the former Dean of Ideology, whom the students, in the first heady days of revolution, demanded be canned. The position was canned, too. Dada remained. She sat in the first row and needed no invitation to speak. (She put me in mind of Yogi Berra, not for her dipsy-doodle syntax—there was no accidental poetry in it—but for the shape of her jaw.) If she got stuck in English, she'd fire off what she meant in Slovak and snap her fingers for a translation. Someone always provided it. No matter whom we discussed—Hawthorne, Twain, Dickinson, Welty—Dada wanted to nail his or her "philosophy," summarize it in a sentence. When I called for further comments, other ways of describing Hawthorne's or Welty's view of humanity, Dada's eyes would narrow and her jaw clench. It was hard for her to entertain the notion that writers, or the characters and dramas they created, were larger or more complex than a simple declarative sentence, especially if the sentence had just come from her. I became fond of the Slovak expression *za'hada*, which means *a mystery*. For example, why was Dada—who did not conduct her courses in English—taking my class? When I asked, she threw me an interesting curve. "*Kde je pes zakopaný*," she said. It meant, literally, "Where the dog is buried": or, as Slovak friends would tell me, "Where the truth begins."

JOSEF WAS STANDING OUTSIDE HIS office, having just returned from Bohemia and a special treatment for his kidney. I told him I was happy to see him back.

"As a man pommeled by science, I share your happiness."

"But you look fine, you really do."

"If I'm left alone, I feel normal, though I am told I should feel otherwise. How is Elizabeth? How are you? Have the police given you your residence cards yet?"

"We're fine . . . and the cards, well, that's a story-in-progress."

He invited me in and closed the door. "The police," he said. "You know, last summer Anna, running across the street in the rain to catch a bus, is struck by a car. Her collarbone is knocked out of line, ribs are bruised, nylon stockings ruined—but please, please, she mumbles, it is her fault, not the driver's; she simply wasn't paying attention under her umbrella." He pulled at his beard. "She visits the police station as required and gives her report, absolving the driver. Yet months later, they are still investigating. Today, at an early hour, they took Anna to the scene of the accident, stopped all traffic downtown, made chalk lines, occupied their stations, gave the signal, and sent her back across the street, at a run, to reenact the moment before the car struck her. The police held stopwatches, were timing her for some reason known only to themselves. Over and over they sent this unathletic, middle-aged professor of British literature running across the street, timing her, refining their art, I suppose, until at length she fell and ruined another pair of stockings. She also bloodied her elbows and knees. We can't help but feel she is under suspicion, but for what?"

THE SUNNIEST MEMBER OF THE English faculty was Slavka. "How are things going, Gary?" I told her I was in pursuit of residence cards and having some trouble, but otherwise all was well. "Really? No other problems?"

"Well, my Fourth Year students and I seem to have lost our lecture room. We meet in the courtyard."

"What will you do when it snows in earnest?'"

"A question raised—timidly—by one or two. I said we could get close and recite Whitman. 'Smile O voluptuous cool-breath'd earth! Smile, for your lover comes.'"

"Your American humor. But tell me, seriously, what is the situation with regard to the residence cards?"

I showed her the last form to be filled out.

"It seems," she said, "they are requesting physical examinations."

I explained that Lizzie and I had complete physicals just before leaving the States—as required by the Fulbright office. "I have Xeroxes of the reports," I said.

"Good," Slavka replied. "I will go with you to the police."

THE OFFICIAL WHO HANDLED RESIDENCE cards had dyed hair that made me think of purple Easter-basket grass. Grape Hair and Slavka had two very long exchanges, the clerk dominating. The gist of the first was that the police *might* accept the U.S. health reports. The question was whether the exam had been complete or only partial; partial was unacceptable. And, too, the reports were too old; thirty days seemed to be the limit, but ours were dated almost exactly three months ago. So Grape Hair needed to phone someone in the ministry to obtain special approval, but the person who could grant such approval was not, she knew, available at this hour. The second long exchange concerned any criminal acts Lizzie or I may have committed since arriving in Czechoslovakia. Grape Hair gave me a form that I needed to take downstairs to the police-station coffee shop and buy a special stamp for. Then we were to fill it out with our personal histories—and then, third, mail it to the Division of Criminal Investigation in Bratislava. If this form came back showing that Lizzie and I were clean, I could bring it to Grape Hair's office for *her* stamp. At that time, she assured

Slavka, her call to the ministry regarding the acceptance or refusal of the medical reports should have been completed.

As Slavka translated, I kept my mouth shut. It wasn't easy. I wanted especially to point out that the medical reports had aged because of Grape Hair's sending me home with a new form to complete every time I came to call. Even Slavka's usual sunny aspect was darkened. But in the coffee shop she brightened again. "Well"—smiling bravely—"everything will turn out fine. Would you care for a snack?"

The café was filing with clerks and liver-faced cops on their mid-morning breaks. We bought the special stamp I needed from the same woman who sold us coffee. Slavka guided me through the personal-history form—except for an item or two in different locations, it was identical to all the others. As I sat there keeping my mouth shut about that and about the need to be declared innocent, I saw Grape Hair come in. She bought three hot dogs. No bread, just the sausages. She sat at a nearby table and dipped her dogs, bite by bite, into a great pool of mustard.

A TALL, SLENDER WOMAN IN HER thirties was waiting for me outside the Requalifiers' classroom. "I missed your fall lectures because I was promised work in Canada. But now is no work. So I am here. I have everything. The big book, your assignments." Her voice seemed thinned by distance, like some I picked up on shortwave radio. She had blonde hair waxed in a kind of rooster comb, red-painted lips more vertical than horizontal— bright as a valentine—and light blue-gray eyes so still they seemed fake. Over a white turtleneck sweater she wore a black T-shirt that said in glittering green: KING OF THE DESERT.

"You are a Russian teacher?"

"Finished."

I told Luba Baranova the fall lectures were not quite over and invited her in. She went to the back row, produced a notebook and pen, sat up straight, and fixed her eyes on me. Not once during class did her expression or position seem to change; she might have been posing for a long camera exposure. At one point I asked if she was following okay, and her eyes turned even flatter, as if I were trying to get more information out of her than she was willing to give. The next week her T-shirt said U.S.A. YANKEE WINNER. The hairdo, the lips, the pen in hand, the stare—all the same. I tried another question—what, in her opinion was the biggest lesson Huck Finn learned? The blue-gray eyes seemed to say: Please, I am here, isn't that enough?

On the day before midyear break, Luba approached me in the hall. HELLO HOLLYWOOD, read this week's shirt. She held up her gradebook, which resembled a passport; all students carried them. "I request your signature," she said. "For my first-semester credit. Or I will lose everything. I must have it today. I pray you."

"Don't pray me. Explain. Why today?"

The eyes didn't move. "I must," she said.

"Look, Luba, I am happy to help you. But why today?"

"My credit. I pray you."

"Okay, look. The day is young. We will meet later."

I went to the English department to see what anyone knew about this woman. In Igor's office, Monika was helping him count books for a private bookshop he ran on campus. They were into it like thieves. I knocked on Josef's door; no response. I found Slavka in, eating a cucumber: "My breakfast. I have been rushing all morning wondering where I am." She had the warmest smile of anyone I'd met in Slovakia, but now, hearing Luba Baranova's request, she turned almost grim. "Yes, I know this situation. You may give her an exam or ask her to write an essay for the first-semester credit."

"But why does she need a signature today?"

"Her problem is not your problem," Slavka said. "Do what you think is best."

At the lecture Luba fixed her look on me as always. I tried to gather up a few threads: a sense of place, the times they are a-changing, who am I? Near the end I went to the padded door and whacked it with my palm, quoting Whitman: "Unscrew the locks from the doors! / Unscrew the doors themselves from their jambs!" It opened. There stood Igor, smiling, up on the balls of his feet. He had the former Russian teachers now, for Didactic, his specialty.

I left. In the hall Luba was suddenly beside me. "Relax," I said. "Don't you want to go to Igor's class?"

"My credit," she said.

"Okay. Five o'clock, in my office?" Meanwhile, I suggested, she might go somewhere quiet, perhaps the library, and prepare.

She shook her head. "No examination can be necessary, because look"—she showed me two pages of exquisite calligraphy detailing the basic facts of Stephen Crane's life, information copied from her text.

"That's fine," I said, "but can you talk about something he wrote?"

"I pray you."

"Please, no praying. Go read. Something *by* Crane, anything, and we'll talk about it. Also anything by Thoreau,

"Thoreau avoided the capitalists."

"Good start. At five o'clock . . ."

"No five o'clock." She was beside me on the stairway to my office. My back was aching. I needed a swim. The pool was open for faculty from four to five. It was quarter to four. I could hear her breathing.

"Okay," I said, stopping, "Who is Huck Finn?"

"A little boy."

"Do you like him?"

"I pray you."

"Please, Luba, go read something."

"'Song of Myself' is a poem by Walt Whitman." She looked at me as if the light had stunned her, maybe even hurt her, then held up her gradebook again. I took it. At the front was a photo taken when she first entered the university, at eighteen or so. Her eyes were regular eyes, youthful, bright, and her lips almost smiled, not yet frozen into the neon heart she walked around with now.

"Listen," I said. "I *will* help you." Her expression softened; she even glanced away and sighed. "Good," I said. "So go to the library and read some passages you can tell me about at five o'clock." I made to return the gradebook, but she didn't want it; she wanted me to take her pen.

"Please, you can sign it now."

My neck was heating up. "Luba, are you listening?"

"Understand me."

"Understand you. Jesus. Where is the dog buried?"

I continued up the ornate handsome lousy stairs and opened my door. She was right beside me. She glanced at Lizzie's new pastels on the walls, then walked to the piano. "Do you play?" I shook my head. "But you have this nice instrument."

"It was just in here."

Suddenly she was seated, playing. Beautifully. Rachmaninoff. The room filled with gorgeous, round, passionate sound. What could be more important?

A Kind of Fable

LIZZIE AND I SETTLE INTO our compartment on the Budapest Express, going to Bratislava. A six-hour ride in the new year—the year the Slovaks and Czechs are officially divorced. We are happy to be leaving Prešov for a while. I open my copy of *Tess of the D'Urbervilles,* and there is Thomas Hardy quoting Whitman:

"Crowds of men and women attired in the usual costumes, / How curious you are to me!"

A young couple enters. *"Dobrý den,"* we all say. Good day. The newcomers each carry a large bottle of Coke; their jackets say LOS ANGELES on the back. They sit side by side. The man opens a book; the woman slings a leg over one of his and watches him read.

Lizzie and I sit across from each other by the window. I try to follow Angel falling in love with Tess, but I'm distracted by the woman beside me stroking her companion's inner thigh. Finally he tells her to sit across from him. She sighs theatrically, feigning great disappointment, but moves away, taking a magazine from her tote bag. On its cover Madonna is almost bare-breasted, her hair, like Luba Baranova's, twisted in a rooster comb.

The train, brakes shrieking, stops in Ružomberok, and in step four young women with big red Nike duffel bags. The Madonna fan quickly moves next to her man. The tallest newcomer sits beside me, the others beside Lizzie. I say, "Basketball," and they all smile and say, "Basketball!" I introduce myself and Lizzie and explain that we're spending a year in Slovakia.

"And what is your opinion of our tiny country?"

"We have seen the Tatras, Slovenský Raj, Banská Bystrica— many places—and find them beautiful," Lizzie says.

Ah, they smile. They are Sylvia, Nora, Bibi, and Susan. Sylvia, the shortest, most talkative one, says, "We make our names easy for you." Then she announces, "I am the playmaker."

"You bring the ball down court," I say, and she nods. "Who is the shooter? You?" I say to Susan beside me.

"They all score!" Sylvia laughs. "I feed them."

Unlike my students, they warm up fast. They are in high school in Ružomberok; they study English, economics, geography, literature; their team is sponsored by a local club that sends them to Italy, Spain, Poland; they're a Junior team, but next year they can play Senior ball if they're good enough. Susan, they say, is good enough right now. In fact, she has played in several Senior games already. Sylvia proudly says that two years ago, at sixteen, Susan was recruited for Ružomberok, brought there from Stara Tura, given an apartment, money to live on. "Oh yes, Susan will be big!" Sylvia promises.

Susan is already at least six feet tall and, I'm guessing, not easily pushed around. Last week, says Sylvia, they were in Valencia. Susan's brother, a student there, came to watch them play. "Yes," Susan says, "maybe I will study in Valencia, too, if I don't sign with a professional team."

"A professional team in Slovakia?" Lizzie asks.

Of course, they all say. In Ružomberok they draw three hundred people a game! Better than in Bratislava, where maybe only fifty come.

"Why is that?" I ask. "It's the capital."

They laugh. Maybe there is nothing else to do in Ružomberok! All four women are relaxed and at ease with us, confident. In Bratislava tomorrow they will play an exhibition against an Austrian team, and they expect to win; afterwards they will enjoy a hot shower, a good meal, and maybe—why not?—some dancing. I am for them, with them, and though I can't watch them play tomorrow because I will be giving a poetry reading in Comenius University, I will be closer to them, I think, than to any of their countrymen.

I ask if the Czech-Slovak split will change things much for them. No, they shrug. I ask if it's better in Slovakia now than three years ago.

"Maybe," says Sylvia.

"Could you travel to Italy and Spain before the revolution?"

"Me? I was too young. But my father—of course." Her father is manager of their club. Before becoming manager, he too was an athlete and could travel anywhere. "But he is not a businessman," she wants to make clear. This is a delicate point, because "manager" in her part of the world now is a complex word: Formerly it meant "important Party functionary"; now it describes, more often than not, a former Communist who emerged from the revolution with money from a strongbox or a secret Swiss account, money he could invest, hence a capitalist, a mover and shaker, perhaps a quick-change artist. (I think of Igor and his private bookshop.) But this is messy territory, nothing like a basketball court, where the lines are clearly drawn and everything is in the open, so we turn our attention to the window. We're passing the town where the delicious Figaro chocolate is made—have we tried it?

We pass another town, where the players say a nuclear reactor sits, boiling away—"the dirtiest anywhere." We pass Stará Turá, where Susan grew up. All of these connections are suddenly bouncing around the compartment like so many loose basketballs: revolution, candy, poison, home. Talk about messy. Well, we don't. We change the subject, focus on Bratislava. We are all eager to arrive and be hosted, honored, distracted by the capital. And, too, Bratislava is only a short hop from Vienna, gateway to the fabulous West.

Yes, Slovakia is difficult to talk about, but so is a rainbow, so is a fish. Maybe that's why none of my colleagues except the Grmelas—who scarcely count because they are Czech and never joined the Party—have invited us into their homes. Things are too much right now—too hopeful, too slippery, too messy. Meeting at the police station is one thing; where one sleeps and perhaps dreams is another. They say, "We must get together and really talk . . . soon"—then look at their watches—"but not today, unfortunately"—and rush to class. It is a refrain, a tic, a speech for a play that doesn't have much development. But the locked-in is everywhere: from the glum silence on city buses to—ironically—the best essay in English (despite its content, it won, I was told, because it had no grammatical errors and was therefore declared perfect) to my perpetually worried Fourth Year students. When I handed out questions at the start of the year and explained we would look for different ways to respond, they said, "Ways? But there is only one way." No ambiguity for them. A poem, a story, or a novel is not a work of imagination reflecting the richness and complexity of the human condition but a document of almost legal shape, a treatise, a blueprint demonstrating something black and something white, and it all means *this . . .* in a sentence or two.

"But why?" I burst out. "I mean why *now?*" They gaze at their hands.

I think of Luba Baranova's remark, "You know, we are used to behaving. Under the Nazis, under the Communists, we were good." I think of Katarina Fetkova, who chairs the English department at the University of Mateja Bela, the school where Party members once went for seminars to keep rigid. She invited me to give a poetry reading. "You will have an attentive audience. We are a rural people—like everywhere in Slovakia—trained not to make noise." Later she said, "Allow me to tell you a fable. There are all these young children who receive very nice treatment, warm attention; even their schools seem cleaner and brighter than schools for older kids. As they grow up, less personal attention is paid to them; they are divided into two basic groups, the clever and the dull, and given their lessons in earnest. The clever will go to university, the dull to trade school, but in either case they will want the same things. It is no accident," Katarina Fetkova said, "that we live as we do."

But once a beautiful moment: I said to my Fourth Year students, "When I appear to be angry with you, I'm really not. I'm only pretending—it's a ruse, an attempt to get you to *talk.*"

A little voice among them said, "It's like us. When we appear to be quiet, we're really not. We're only pretending to be quiet."

The train makes one more stop before Bratislava. The Madonna fan and her man depart, and we're joined by a woman wearing a new leather jacket and carrying a big cardboard box that Sylvia helps her settle on the floor. The woman, about forty, is all smiles when she hears English being spoken. She tells Sylvia to tell us that she gets English on her TV every day now because she has a dish. We all acknowledge her good fortune.

Now she wants to open her box and show the Americans something. *Here! Look!* She takes out a handful of dolls—each maybe three inches tall—made from cornhusks. At first I think they are little girls wearing some festive Slovak head-wrap, but no, they are Jesus dolls, two hundred of them, and the yellow head-wrap is a halo. She, her husband, and their son spent all week constructing them. The son helped because he wishes to buy a motorcycle with his share, the mother says, smiling, proud of his ambition. She is taking the dolls to Bratislava for the tourists. Are we tourists? Sylvia explains that I am a visiting professor, and the woman says, "*Ano, ano,*" yes, yes, and puts away her dolls.

I ask how long she has been making them. She holds up three fingers: three years. And every week she can travel to the city and trade them for designer jeans, leather jackets, a satellite dish, even a motorcycle. She sinks back in her seat. "Life," she sings in English, "is A-okay." I catch Sylvia's eye. She who has three hundred Ružomberok fans come watch her dribble a ball, she whose father manages a club that sponsors a team that can travel to Italy or Spain—that has been able to travel outside the country for years—she shrugs and gives me a grin that says, I think, *So what else is new?*

WHERE TO?

ON THE BUS THAT WOULD take us into Poland there were five other passengers, all smugglers. They'd come down to Slovakia early that morning, loaded up with vodka and hair coloring in Prešov, and as we rode north, four of them were busy working to hide the stuff, to avoid paying Polish import tax. Lizzie and I watched.

The one who wasn't fussing was feeling good. He stood in the aisle combing his black cowlick and sang a song about swans. The young woman who resembled Ingrid Bergman fixed a pillow under her sweater to look pregnant, then got out needles and a partially finished rug; she spread her knitting over the sackful of hair-coloring boxes in the seat beside her, a wary expression in her eyes but otherwise the picture of serene budding motherhood.

The other three Poles were jittery as squirrels. The thin one had packaged his hair coloring in a crate that resembled an air-conditioning unit and placed it under a rear seat. Though he sat near the front, after every bump or sharp turn he would hustle back to check on the crate, nudge it with his foot to line it up just so.

The heavy woman in the first seat, catty-corner from the driver, had both vodka and hair dye. She spent much of the journey to the border telling the driver how good the coloring was, holding a box for him to see. Look, she said, beautiful red tint, very natural—and at such a good price. She regretted now the vodka—it took up too much room. Look, she said, didn't the driver agree the coloring was beautiful? He said, "*Tak, tak*," Yes, yes, but kept his eyes on the road. She had her vodka in a suitcase and the hair coloring in two duffels piled atop it, everything snug beside her, and she patted the luggage and cooed as if she had a pet in there that needed comforting.

Finally, the man with the mustache—the least organized of all—stood in the aisle as if in despair over his two jumbo suitcases of vodka. An hour out of Prešov he was still debating whether to leave them in their separate seats or to push them under. Too full, too full, he kept telling the man who was feeling good. His eyes drooped like a basset hound's.

Back in Prešov he'd helped me out. I approached the driver to buy my tickets. "*Dokad*," the driver said. Where to? He told me how much to Krosno in złotys. I offered crowns. "Polish bus, Polish money," he said. I didn't have any. He shrugged. "*Szkoda.*" Too bad.

I knew the exchange rate, more or less, and offered extra crowns. He shook his head; he couldn't be bothered. He was waiting, I reckoned, for dollars. I was about to pull some out when the man with the mustache said, "Here." He handed me 100,000 złotys and asked for 200 crowns. I was happy to let him make a good commission so I could save my dollars for Poland.

On the bus, he asked if I could carry two bottles across the border. I said sure. Why were we going to Krosno? I explained we were going beyond it, to Rzeszów, spending the night, then going to a small village, Ostrów, where my *dziadek,* Stefan Szostak, was born.

When the man who was feeling good heard I was a Polish grandson, he immediately brought me a plastic glass filled with vodka and orange pop. He was Marek, he said. We told him our names. He said, "No Gary, no Elizabeth. Gariego, Elzbieta." Then—beaming—"Chicago!" We told him no, Iowa. But next year Idaho. "Idaho? Idaho? *Dlaczego*?" Why? For the mountains, we told him.

He smiled and said Elzbieta needed vodka. I told him no, only me, and put my hand on Lizzie's stomach. *Dziecko,* child.

He slapped me on the back and insisted we toast the child, Elzbieta, grandfather Szostak, Chicago, the mountains, the

USA, Poland, and finally this good Polish bus. "Not bad," he said, "is life."

The man with the mustache, who'd eased away during all this, now returned. He had two more bottles he wished me to carry over: "You can do it, no problem." I said okay. Then he showed me a bus ticket to Rzeszów, saying I would need forty thousand złotys for it. I counted out enough crowns to trade, plus a tip. He shook his head sadly; he had no more złotys. I handed back the two bottles. He looked shocked: Marek roared, then said, "Greedy boy." He waved Mustache away and produced the złotys I needed.

As the bus slowed for the border crossing, the driver barked, "Pivo! Pivo!" Marek got two bottles of Czech pilsner from his bag and handed them up. When the Polish guard came to the driver's window, the bottles were stealthily slipped out. He returned to his shed; the five smugglers sat up straight and kept their eyes dead ahead, as if to show how good they could be. He came back with a clipboard and had the driver step out and open the storage area. Then the guard boarded the bus. He walked slowly to the rear, saying nothing. The heavy woman looked in a small mirror and put on fresh lipstick, watching him; as he passed, the knitter belched, patting her stomach, clacking her needles; the thin man bent to tie his shoelace and looked back along the aisle to see how his fake air-conditioner would fare; Marek produced a small black book and a thoughtful expression; Mustache sat with his feet on the two enormous suitcases that he'd finally decided to push to the floor. The guard only glanced at us. He finished his stroll and waved us on. After the driver crossed into Poland, just out of sight of the border station, he pulled over, and the smugglers scrambled out as if the bus were on fire. Cigarettes were lit and glasses filled. By God, they'd done it! For only two bottles of Czech beer and a presentation of respect.

The next day a bus delivered Lizzie and me to a country crossroads. "Ostrów," the driver said. In a circle of speckled shade made by a single oak, a dozen mares and colts stood muzzle to muzzle while a man measured bellies, examined teeth. Other men watched. Judging from the shapes of jaws and noses and full, unbroken eyebrows, I reckoned they were all kin to me. They took us in, briefly, shyly. A breeze came and pushed over green hay in the field beside us, and then the grass sprung up straight again. I could have hung around that tree for as long as I did my grandfather's orchard and creek and forge, unconcerned with time, simply waiting for the next thing, but after a while we walked up the road in the spring air toward a lone house.

It was a café. We ate bean soup and bread. I asked the teenaged girl serving us if any Szostaks lived in Ostrów. She shrugged. Then, leading us outside, she pointed to a wooden steeple rising above a cluster of trees. The village center. I asked about a *cmentarz*. She said, "*Tak*," and pointed to a rise just up the road.

We started for the cemetery. Lizzie sighed when a stork flew over, flapping and clacking. She said, "I'm sorry, Dr. G, it's almost too damn much." Beans and wheat grew in fields on either side of us, and in the distance, across from the cemetery, a white horse, a plow, and a man—the reins looped around his neck—cut fresh furrows, like waves, in a soft brown, almost perfectly round hill.

The treeless graveyard seemed far too big, too populous, for such a small village. Months before, in a reference book on patronymic surnames, I found Szostak and Szostek, good Polish names. I also found Shostack, Shustak, Shostag (East German), and Šesták (Czech). All were derived, the book said, from the Belorussian Shostakovich. There was conjecture that the names were connected to the word *shast,* six, possibly denoting a person with six fingers on one hand. Still I was finding no Szostaks or anything close. When I looked up to stretch my back, the farmer and his beautiful white horse continued to cut their wavelike furrows in the brown hill. I wanted to go ask his name, and his horse's. Then Lizzie, in a far row, said she'd found one. Maria Szostak something, who died in 1933 or 1938. We found more, pressing our fingers against the fading letters and numbers as if tracing them into the soft stone.

THE VILLAGE CENTER CONSISTED OF a simple, bark-colored wooden church, a few shade trees, and a packed-dirt area where horse carts could park. We approached a man lying in his empty grain cart under a tree, having a smoke. Waving my arm around, I asked, "Szostak?" He sat up, looked at the sky, then smiled and pointed down a lane to a barn. There, Lizzie and I found a pink-cheeked old man searching his tool bench. I asked him, "Szostak?" He glanced at our bags twice, then took off on a hard dirt path.

"Are we supposed to follow him?" Lizzie asked. I guessed we were.

We met a man on a bicycle, at whom our guide fired some Polish. The man got off his bike, let it fall; now the two of them led us. We came to a stream and walked beside it. We were in a forest, though here and there a weathered house abruptly revealed itself. I thought of the Roma settlement below Šariš Castle. Our guides stopped at a little house held up, it appeared, by cherry and apple trees. The cyclist knocked; a man came out and said he was Andrzej, grandson of Maria Szostak. He looked so much like my uncle Joe I had trouble making verbs, the possessive. Reduced to nouns and pointing, I got across that I too was grandson of a Szostak.

"Moment." He went back in and returned with a handsome carved chair, one clearly intended for special occasions. He set it under a cherry tree for Lizzie. He then brought out three more like it: one for me, one for himself, and one that our two guides shared by sitting sideways with their elbows on their knees. Then Andrzej and I, using American place names and mainly Polish nouns (my plunge into pidgin had infected him), struggled and thought and slapped our foreheads and clapped our hands. "Moment!" He brought out an envelope, very old, bearing a Chicago return address. Everyone studied the writing, the stamps. Stamps licked by my great-uncle Jacob—brother of Maria and Stefan. The bicyclist grabbed the sides of his head and exclaimed, in English, "Fantastic!" Andrzej gazed into the canopy of limbs shading us and could not stop smiling.

That night Lizzie and I stayed in the Hotel Cukrownia—the Hotel Sugar—which sat beside a sugar-beet factory five kilometers from Ostrów. It was a workers' hotel. We paid 110,000 złotys, about six dollars. I recorded this in my notebook, along with the detail that next to our room a worker fried eggs in a communal kitchen for his dinner.

I couldn't remember asking my mother very much about Grandpa when I was growing up. Not that I wasn't curious; but almost always there seemed to be this response in my family when I asked a question: "Just watch—and see." I was instructed by people who used their hands, who laid down a level and followed the bubble, who wiped a knife blade in the up position, not the down—so you won't hurt yourself, see? But once I heard words that were better than usual—words that didn't end when my mother stopped saying them: "He came from the Old Country, a handsome educated young man—oh yes, very smart—and strong as a bull—he had to be, because of all the troubles he went through. They were always fighting over there, those Polish kings, those Russian Cossacks. On horses, with swords!" I had seen Grandpa drape complicated harnesses on his big-shouldered Belgians, seen him lift red-tipped pokers from the fiery forge, and I believed everything she told me. I still believed her, collecting my facts.

I knew the dangers of facts, their insistence on making a straight line, a balanced weight, an answer the teacher will give you a star for and that you can tuck away in the place where you store your answers and stars. And maybe forget about. I did not want that. I did not want the exact number of clacking bones in a skeleton—I wanted what Joseph Conrad wanted, the questions, the mysteries, the imperfections and contradictions of the human heart. "A man's real life," he wrote, "is that accorded to him in the thoughts of other men by reason of respect or natural love." I respected my grandfather, but did I love him? Or did I love those images of him in his blacksmith shop, gazing at the sky in his bee-sweetened orchard, opening his book in the honeyed glow of a kerosene lamp at a table we all moved away from? "The dead," Conrad said, "can live only with the exact intensity and quality of life imparted to them by the living."

My mother was old enough to remember the day he came home from Ford's foundry, splashed on by molten steel. He took his family north from Detroit and became a farmer. The summers I was eight, nine, and ten I followed him around. We never exchanged a word. But then one summer I elected to stay in Flint and play baseball. That August he died and was buried on my eleventh birthday. Almost two decades later Grandma told me, "Korzeniowski, always reading this Korzeniowski, even on his last day." Trembling, I asked if I could see that last book. She said no, because just before Mr. Savage, the undertaker, closed the coffin, she put it under Grandpa's arm. All those years Steve Szostak had read Joseph Conrad, in Polish—even on his last day. But how would I know that? I knew other things. That he stood in a driving rain and raised his fist at the heavens for drowning his beans. That he sat me on the hay wagon, between his knees, and gave me the reins. Up and down the field we raced until Grandma rushed out, *her* fist, her skirts, and the Polish flying, afraid I would be hurt . . . and he, his hands over mine, helped me steer the wagon around and around her. He called my grandmother *Nelly*. He had a mare of the same name and waded into the creek with her, took off his shirt, bathed his scarred shoulders and back while she waited. In 1902, the year of their marriage, Grandma wears a rose in her hair. She is sixteen, looking out at the world like a young woman who's spent the afternoon in her flower garden, alone, thinking how lovely everything is, how temporary, and just at that moment when happiness and melancholy compete most for her heart, the photographer snaps her. And later, in his studio, applies to her full and youthful cheeks a subtle blush.

In the Hotel Sugar, I stood at the window seeing stars, their random toss. I also saw a circle of sun-freckled farmers, a plowman and his beautiful white horse cutting wave-like furrows in a round hill. A stork flew over our heads, speaking to us. "How do you feel?" I asked. "At the beginning," Lizzie said. We sat in special chairs under apple and cherry trees planted by a man with whom I shared a name we found on some fading stones. He couldn't stop shaking his head in wonder. I wondered, before we went away from those trees making speckled shadows in my wife's hair, if I would ever again see such bright shade. We had spent only a short while there, a blink in time; it was enough and not nearly enough.

Looking Out

Taped on the wall in front of my desk was the following exchange:

"Poof, you're dead."

"I don't want to be dead. I want to look out the window."

I overheard this the summer my daughter Margaret was six and playing with her friend James, the poof guy, who was five. I served them lunch, told them a story. I pushed them on Margaret's swing—it was a good one, a long sweep between two giant pine trees, and every kid who ever had that ride toward the sky gripped the ropes and wanted to keep on riding. Many things, of course, happened that day. But what I was held by as the year 2001 neared its end was the little scrap above my desk.

Looking out the window, I saw my Gala apple tree, bare but for the ripe fruit hanging in the early November morning sun. Thousands of pine and red fir gathered near and far, the peaks of the Gospels at the farthest reach beginning to snow up. There was frost on the ground around the Gala, depressions in the grass where deer spent the night. My gray barn cat, Yah teh, sat on a rock above the frost, warming herself. Her head swiveled a sly turn toward me, and her green eyes shone. I remembered climbing on a branch in my grandfather's apple orchard, to better watch him as he sat in the high timothy gazing at the sky.

What was he looking for? He would sit there a long time— *had* been sitting there a long time, an eternity. I am nine or ten. We will never exchange a word, he and I, for I don't understand Polish and he speaks, when he does speak, nothing else. He will smile, pat me on the head, give me a leg up so I may sit on Nelly, his big brown Belgian. But not one word. And yet words, I will discover, will bring us closer than I can ever guess.

Miles Davis once asked John Coltrane why he took such long solos. Coltrane said, "It takes me that long to get everything in."

How to get everything in?

A couple months before September 11, my smoky-eyed dog, Henry, and I were into our poky jog through the timber, of an evening a body could haul itself uphill or down and feel pretty fine either way—and I said, "Henry, where do you reckon all the women have taken themselves these piney-sweet nights under such moons turning the everlasting yearning ever so keenly near? Henry," I said, "you don't need to answer that woeful wonder; it's just a thought I thought I ought to throw out—" and he didn't.

I don't worry about sounding foolish. It somehow clears the air sometimes, puts me in my place. Or did. After 9-11 I became less good at it. More and more, I spent time looking out. I stood by the river where it made a large curl, an almost perfect question mark without the dot, and picked out the stars in the water. Were they really there? I saw them, but science reminded me they had already left.

I leave, too. I go home, hungry for flavor, and savor fresh salmon, red peppers roasted with lots of garlic. Then in my leather chair beside the woodstove, I reread "In the Ravine," a Chekhov story. When my eyes tire, I go upstairs and crawl under my goose-down comforter. If I am lucky, nothing will come to keep me awake and wondering about all that cool, starry silence above my skylight.

"EVERY DAY I GET CUTER and meaner."

Margaret again. She said this at breakfast, out of the blue, during one of her visits. I was too delighted—and caught—to ask for a gloss. Instead, I asked if she could eat another pancake. No, she said, she had work to do and didn't want to feel *too* good.

My wall of scraps grew larger, the days shorter. During the school year I had Margaret every other weekend. On one of these she presents me with a drawing of a purple butterfly—the eight-by-ten sheet of paper cannot contain the full expanse of its wings, and I must imagine where they end. She says, "You need this, Dad." I assume she means both the parts I see and the parts beyond. I add the butterfly to my wall, next to a still of Marilyn Monroe resting her cheek on Clark Gable's arm in *The Misfits.*

Is Margaret crying? I go up to her room. Quietly I stand by the open door and watch her reading to her "children"—a dozen dolls and stuffed animals gathered in a circle on the floor around her. She is reading from Laura Ingalls Wilder's *By the Shores of Silver Lake,* the part where Laura's dog, Jack, old and gray, lay on his blanket "and did not stir." Margaret's eyes glisten. She does not see me.

A friend of mine, a doctor, once handed me a raw filet mignon as we stood beside his grill. "Choice, boneless," he said, "just like the human heart." He laughed. He didn't really want to be just a doctor, he said; he wanted to be a writer, too. "I tried and tried," he said, "but unlike Chekhov and Somerset Maugham and Walker Percy and Bill Williams—those lucky bastards—I couldn't get past the meat." He took back the filet, winked, and without missing a beat, dropped it on the hot grill, saying, "How do you like your boneless protein?"

Years before that moment at Margaret's door, I came home one afternoon to another house, and heard sobbing upstairs in Gretchen's room. Gretchen was nine then. I went up and found her on her bed clutching *Charlotte's Web,* open to where Charlotte's children are sailing off on the wind, crying, "Good-bye, good-bye, good-bye" to the pig Wilbur.

I took her in my arms, feeling her wet cheek on my neck. I can still feel it. Then twenty years of departures go by like nothing.

Really, like nothing?

Clichés often come to our lips so quickly because that's what we want—a quick fix to fill the emptiness. But they don't fix anything. The rescue, the real gathering up, takes the kind of time Coltrane's response to Miles Davis hints at, I reckon. And *solo* is a good, hard, useful word here. Or as Joseph Conrad had Marlow say in *Heart of Darkness*, "We live, as we dream—alone."

A professor of philosophy wanted to argue with me about those six hard little words. "Do you mean to tell me," he said, "that the wife I've lived with for thirty years, thirty loving years, hasn't *shared* my life, my dreams—and I hers?"

I said to him that they were Conrad's words, not mine, but, yes, I did subscribe to them.

"Nonsense," the professor said. "Where's the heart in all that?"

"Maybe Conrad's point," I said.

"Oh?"

"Your wife has her heart, you have yours."

Our host came by with a tray of finger food (we were at a reception following my poetry reading) and the professor said to me, "Try the cayenne meatballs—maybe *they'll* warm you up." Then he turned away to join another conversation.

The professor's reaction to Conrad's sentence, I'd guess, started a long time ago, perhaps at the moment he was first kissed by the woman with whom he would share his dreams. I am very much in favor of kisses; I know they can go deep, far deeper than our commentaries on them. Which doesn't mean we will keep our mouths shut. "The last good kiss / you had was years ago," the poet Richard Hugo laments. "Give me a kiss to build a dream on," a popular song implores. "Shut up and kiss me, stupid," countless pulp fiction molls have said to their big lugs. (That last line is even better without the comma.)

Gretchen now teaches college English in Iowa. She has two children of her own, Gabriel and Joanna, both readers like their mother. Iowa is a three-day drive from Idaho, where Margaret and I live. Three long days from Pacific time, through Mountain, to Central.

"HELLO, CENTRAL, GIVE ME HEAVEN."

Where did that hopeful chirp come from? An old movie? I see telephone operators connecting callers, plugging lines into their switchboard, their hair tied in high cones, their painted lips "bee-stung." I once dated a girl whose mother, a former telephone operator, *had* looked like the Hollywood version, proudly possessing a photo to prove it. She could also sit at her piano and sing any number of songs from the war years. "Don't Sit Under the Apple Tree (With Anyone Else But Me)" and "I'll Be Seeing You" and so on. The good war, people say, their expression often finding room for the dreamy.

A dream solo that led to "The Gig"—

> They invited me in, then
> asked what I played.
> I said horn. They

handed me one with a long cord
hanging down. They said
sample it, man. I
put the small round end
to my mouth and blew—
it was okay. Unusual
but okay. Then the guy
on sax tapped out one, two,
one, two, three, and we started.
He was good, he grew large
wings, wings and a deep concern.
Everyone stopped, including me.
The question seemed to be:
Where were we?
I felt bad. My timing
was slow, the sound
I pushed out full of
wet air, farty.
And that cord kept
getting underfoot.
But I wasn't going to
make excuses. My horn
was a damn lamp
with a yellow shade.
My lips were sore.
So what? This was the gig.
Let's go, I said. Let's play.

Our dreams sometimes cut such slapstick figures. And sometimes, as here, I can make a rough translation of one, though never a transcription, an exact copy. My lips *are* sore. But from too few, not too many, kisses.

"In the Ravine," the Chekhov tale I'm reading, is set in the village of Ukleevo, which lies in a ravine, "a wretched hole." When strangers ask what is this place, they are told: it's "where the deacon ate all the caviar at the funeral." Chekhov explains that the old deacon spotted the caviar at once and ate "greedily; people nudged him, tugged at his arm, but he seemed petrified with enjoyment: felt nothing, and only went on eating. He ate up all the caviar . . . four pounds in the jar." Ten years go by, "the deacon had long been dead, but the caviar was still remembered. Whether life was so poor here or people had not been clever enough to notice anything but that unimportant incident . . . anyway the people had nothing else to tell about the village of Ukleevo."

But Chekhov has much to tell about this village. To use my physician friend's term, he gets past the meat—or in this case the caviar—to a heartbreaking, simple story that cannot be summarized. I tried to summarize it once, to a teacher who works with poor children, and is the mother of a son—a woman who has endured great hardship and come through—but I was failing miserably. My enthusiasm for the story wasn't enough; my wish for her to see how we, all of us, were connected to its truths wasn't enough. I was offering a plastic rose, not the real thing, and stopped, saying, "This is no good, you have to read it." I promised to deliver the story, but before I could, she called and said she could no longer see me. There were too many differences between us, she said. We lived in two different worlds, she said.

More than once, out walking in the timber, I have thought of how often one story leads to another, how they seem to circle and flirt and borrow back and forth, and comment on each other, sometimes crooning, sometimes hooting, challenging, sometimes speaking in noises whose meaning we feel but cannot cipher right away.

Now I think of those summers of my boyhood when I was delivered up north to my Polish grandparents' farm. I fished and swam in the creek. I jumped from the barn's beams into its

stores of pillowy hay. I searched the woods for berries and animal tracks, and I rode on the backs of my grandfather's team
of Belgians, Nelly and Prince. Some days, from a good perch in
an apple tree, I watched my grandfather sit on the rim of the
orchard floor and gaze at the sky. He sat, it seemed, without
moving, and for the longest time. What was he looking at, this
man whose big hands could smoothly squeeze milk from a cow,
shape a plow's blades brought red-hot from his forge, pat me
on the head for a chore performed well, turn the pages of a
book he pulled from under his shirt every night after dinner?
No one in my family read books so avidly—certainly no men.

The summer I turned eleven and chose baseball over the
farm, he died. He was buried on my eleventh birthday. Usually
it comes back to me as I'm picking apples in my orchard—though
sometimes when I'm doing nothing to encourage it—how almost
two decades later my grandmother said to me that when she
found grandpa in his orchard on that last awful day, he was
clutching yet another book by Joseph Conrad. Only she used
his Polish name, Korzeniowski.

I WAS DRIVING ACROSS THE COUNTRY in my pickup, giving poetry
readings at colleges along the way, when those four airplanes
were taken over by terrorists on September 11th. At the time
I did not think of the terrorists as clichés. It's hard not to, now.
The fanatics of the Inquisition, of the Salem witch trials, of the
Taliban—not to mention the bully, wife beater, rapist, racist—
aren't they all stopped and self-held at one hateful level? To
recognize another, others, to consider, weigh, debate, doubt,
pause, wonder, to simply look out the window—no.

But why?

No.

On September 12th I arrived at a small college in Price,
Utah. I asked my host if she thought we'd get much of an

audience. She said she didn't know—maybe her twenty poetry students?

That night I read to seven times that number, including faculty, administration, townspeople, and children. Several came up afterward and thanked me as if I had specifically made the journey to Price because of the events of the previous day, to help bring thoughts back to normal things. They were numbed, drained, *tired*, many said, of watching those planes crash over and over and over into the Twin Towers. The TV images, it occurred to me, had become the worst kind of clichés, if there is a worst kind, and there must be when so much death and damage is caused and all that can be articulated is a repetition of the obvious.

I am writing these words with a pencil on sheets of paper whose reverse sides contain a story about a family that has broken up. The sheets of paper came out flawed from a copy machine—the lines too close, margins erratic—but I saved them because they were still useful. The nuns taught me years ago not to waste paper. Not to waste anything. Anyway, the point of this paragraph, I think, is that my handwriting has become almost childish lately, large and sprawling, and I erase a lot, and misspell the simplest words.

Perhaps this large awkward hand wants to take me back to a time when I first began making sentences—in my Big Chief tablet at St. Joseph's School in northern Michigan. A time of all-time and no-time. When the roughly soft, blue-lined tablet sheets smelling like my pencil and desktop and the nun's brown wool habit, and the sandwich wrapped in brown paper inside my little tin lunchbox, and the clean, cream-colored wood being cut by the big blue buzz saw in my German grandfather's lumberyard after school, and the discarded chunk I took away whose round piney knot slipped in and out like a cork, and the sun-sparkled minnow I scooped from the creek behind our house with my empty Dixie Cup, and whose eyes never blinked, and my puzzlement at this, and my collie, Brownie, choosing to sleep outside even after it began to snow, and reaching under the white mound in the morning to feel him fur-warm in his own igloo—a time, I mean to say, when all these things could somehow move and stay and hold me from day to day and season to season in one smooth mysterious clear gathering forever.

I still use Big Chief tablets, but they are harder and harder to find. Perhaps because children are moved younger and younger to the computer. It is powerful, the computer, but not nearly as powerful as the rose, or a child's smile, the sweet confusions of first love, the intimacy of memory and desire. Machines are still only machines, and yet we are capable of bowing before these arrangements of wires and artificial lights and chips of plastic that go zip as if they knew the exact route to the interior, and back. No need to drop crumbs of bread on the path to remember the way.

An angel made of twigs stood on my bookcase. Often I looked at this figure and felt both happy and helpless. I once tried making something out of such a predicament, the attempt leading only to a fragment:

> I know the body is a loose translation.
> The wings, the face
> are simply willows and shoots,
> reminders of the wayward murmur
> of a river rushing by,
> the silvery cry a veery can't help—
> the man and woman who brought their child here,
> so full in their frail hearts
> they could explain nothing, only
> gather a few sticks, all they could carry,
> and hurry to follow the willowy girl
> flapping her arms.

AT A DINNER PARTY IN late September, 2001, in a large barn warmly refigured into a home, the easy cordiality at the table prompted a poet to spontaneously raise her glass. "To happiness," she beamed.

All of us understood at once, I think, what her toast really was: a combination wish, prayer, and reaffirmation of a mighty pursuit in response to the shocking events of twelve days before. We hadn't talked much about them here; we'd had enough for a while; though we did need what the poet was calling for: tranquility of a higher order, goodness, a thing so dear that it's the centerpiece of our country's most cherished document whose author nearly missed it. Jefferson had first written, *life, liberty, and the protection of property.* Even Ben Franklin, our most practical forefather, knew that last part simply wasn't enough.

So we raised our glasses, gladly. Teachers, poets, a fiction writer, an engineer, a musician, an artist, a gardener, a breeder of horses. Two of us were transplants from Britain, one from Denmark, all were serious readers. Happiness became our coat of arms and marching tune and hearth.

"Onward!"

"Indeed!"

In the midst of this glow, I remembered Tolstoy's sober beginning of *Anna Karenina:* "All happy families are alike but an unhappy family is unhappy after its own fashion." I quoted it now, as a reminder, perhaps more to myself than to anyone else, that happiness does not come easy and cheap.

"No," my fellow poet said, "I'm tired of that. Of knocking happy families."

"He isn't. He's only saying—"

"I know what he's saying, and I say *you* have written happy poems," she said. "I have, too. I don't get it, this dwelling on—"

"But—"

"I'm tired of it."

How had we come to this jumpy, unhappy pass? Surely we were on the same side—the side opposite clichés. Which was where Tolstoy stood, along with so many others who have tried to describe what's true about the world, what goes deep, matters. But that wasn't the problem; as any good cook or comic or batter in the box would tell us, we needed—and soon—to get our timing back. Then we could get on with it.

I'm glad to say that before the evening was over, the two poets in that refigured barn in the woods of northern Michigan got their timing back. And embraced. This was not a given; poets are as capable as anyone of harboring, nursing, even thriving on, bitterness. For years, a lifetime. How is this possible? Are we not devoted to song? To delight? To what moves us closer to our best selves? The Slovaks have an expression for such questions: *za'hada.* This may be translated: *a mystery, a mystery surrounds us.* Another possible answer is: the pursuit of happiness is exactly that fierce and that vulnerable.

Grigory Petrovitch Tsybukin, a clever successful tradesman, has two sons. Anisim, the older, is a policeman and seldom home; Stephan works in his father's shop but is not much help because he is deaf and in weak health. He is married to Aksinya, a woman of great energy and ambition, who *is* good in the shop. Old Tsybukin's eyes glow when he watches her scurry from one task to another, often wishing that Anisim had such a wife. He later buys a parcel of land where she builds a thriving brickyard. Anisim marries Lipa, a poor peasant girl who is beautiful, sings like a bird, and is all but ignored by her busy husband. She gives birth to their son, Nikifor, "a tiny, thin, pitiful little baby." She adores him. Her husband, it turns out, has been counterfeiting roubles, is caught and sent to prison. Tysbukin, in deep gloom, cries out, "As long as I live, the family must not break up." He makes a special provision in his will. "My son is gone, but my grandson is left." Aksinya hears of this, hears talk that it's *her* brickyard that Nikifor will inherit. She goes into a rage that does not stop until, in the laundry room, she throws Lipa's boiling water on the boy. "After this was heard such a scream as had never been heard before in Ukleevo." The boy dies, Aksinya gains control of the house, and, as Chekhov leaves them, Lipa and Tsybukin are seen walking their separate journeys we know not where.

This can only mean very much if you know what's missing.

Margaret and I were at the stove making applesauce from the Galas. Her job was to add cinnamon and ginger and maple syrup. I asked if she'd seen any airplanes on TV crashing into buildings. (Her mother had a television set; I didn't.) Margaret was busy with her measuring cup and spoons; my question didn't seem to interest her. I said if she ever saw anything on TV that bothered her and wanted to talk about it, we could, okay?

"Okay."

Earlier, in the orchard, I was picking, and she was holding the sack. I'd planted the Gala, plus a Jonathan and two plum trees, when she was a baby. She knew this story and liked to hear it at times like this.

"I planted these trees because when your mom told me we were going to *have* you, we were walking beside the Danube River in Budapest, Hungary, which is a very old, romantic city, and I was carrying a bag of apples and plums, and I was so excited hearing about *you* that I put the bag on my head and danced around and spilled everything. I promised your mom that when we got home to Idaho I would plant an orchard of apples and plums."

Margaret smiled; I had told the story right.

"Should we leave some on the tree for the animals?" she said.

"That's what we do."

"Yup."

A few days later I looked up from my desk and saw a deer under the tree, and just above her, on a branch, a flicker. At first I thought the deer, most improbably, was wearing a fancy hat. When I laughed out loud at my goofy vision, they both turned toward my window; for sure the doe gave me a long look, and I imagined the woodpecker did, too. In fact, I already had a story started about the unusual friendship a deer, a bird, and a little girl had formed for each other, for when Margaret came to help me out with the hard parts.

Something Clear and True

For Stanley W. Lindberg, 1939-2000

Below the room where I write, way down, I can see the South Fork of the Clearwater rushing black and white, and above it, in the distance, the knuckled peaks of the Gospels softened by snow. A little while ago I looked through a folder—letters going back twenty years. Stan and I met only four times, but it feels like more. We talked on the phone I don't know how many times. "Listen to this," he once said, "Zimmer renewed his subscription—and at the bottom of the form wrote 'Stan Lindberg eats spiders.'" He roared. More recently he asked if I had caught all the trout in my neighborhood, because one of the many things he *planned* to do was fish Idaho—as soon as he got back in shape. "And I want to eat them! No catch and release."

Paul Zimmer "introduced" us, in October of 1978. I had sent Paul a copy of a short story I just finished—"Sleepy Time Gal"—and Paul, then director of the University of Georgia Press, delivered it to Stan at *The Georgia Review* and—as Stan wrote to me—"insisted that I read it right away (even though I've got manuscripts here going back to May). And I'm glad he did . . ."

The first time we met in person, I was in Athens to give a reading at the university, and Paul took me over to Stan's house. Just before we arrived, Paul, pulling at his chin, warned, "Please be *careful* around Lindberg—he wrestled in college—he's nobody to fool with." Wondering how to prepare myself for I couldn't guess what, I was greeted warmly by a man who smiled generously and often, who invited me out to see his garden, who identified two or three unseen birds from the songs that came our way.

Everybody—no, not everybody—knows that Stan Lindberg was a remarkably gifted editor. And a very sensitive guy. I sent him a story two years ago—"Below the Gospels"—about a couple in Idaho who have a child late in life, not unlike Margaret's mother and me. They lose their child to a mountain lion. Stan called me and, his voice tentative, asked how I was . . . how the family was.

"We're fine."

"Everyone's okay? Your daughter?"

"Sure, we're all fine."

"I'm glad to hear it. And by the way, we'd like to keep the story."

The second time we met, also in Athens, was for a big party honoring *The Georgia Review* for winning the National Magazine Award for Fiction. Mary Hood, Lee K. Abbott, and I were asked to read as the authors of the stories that made up the winning entry. Stan arranged for Ray Andrews, the novelist from Georgia, to introduce me. This was a great, wonderful surprise. Ray and I had been college roommates at Michigan State, and only recently had got back in touch after twenty-eight years. Out of the blue Ray had sent me a letter explaining what had happened to him—which was quite a lot and a lot of it good—and at the party I felt especially honored and lucky for Stan's having involved Ray in that happy event.

Four years later when Ray ended his life, it was Stan who called me with the news. I met him at the memorial service in Atlanta. I told some stories about Ray and me in college, like going to the Chicago Art Students' Ball our freshman year dressed only in penny loafers and caveman leopard skins that his brother Benny had found for us, and in the wee hours after the ball getting lost, taking the wrong train—to Milwaukee—with no money, and wondering how we'd get back to East Lansing.

"But look what you got," Stan said.

I wish I had some stories about fishing with this guy in Idaho. Getting lost in the sweet, pine-scented mountain air, in the river's flow. Tossing our lines out, and out again. *It's what we do,* he might say. *Trying to catch something clear and true. So we can keep it.*

Journeys We're On

I was on the phone with my cousin Leonard, a retired draftsman living on a lake in Florida. I told him I was writing a memoir about our grandfather, Steve Szostak, and wanted to ask a few questions.

"Oh, man," he groaned, as if I were crazy. "But go ahead, fire away."

I fired away, he made listening noises, and then, suddenly, "Look, this is old stuff. Come down to Florida. I'll take you fishing, tell you a *good* story. I've got all this material I've wanted to put in a book for years. I just need somebody to, you know, fix up the sentences."

During his rebellious youth, Leonard dropped out of high school and hitchhiked from Detroit to Sunset Boulevard to sit in Hollywood's fabled Schwab's drugstore, where fetching sixteen-year-old Judy Turner, he'd heard, was spotted sipping a soda and became movie star Lana Turner. My starry-eyed cousin sat at that same fountain for a week hoping a brand-new luminous ball of gas would be discovered; but he ran out of soda money and had to hitchhike home. Fix up the sentences in that kind of story, he meant.

Almost everyone I contacted who had known Steve longer than I had—other cousins, aunts, my mother—at some point would turn fanciful, veering off, circling, correcting, coming abruptly to a hard place and starting over.

I was well into *My Grandfather's Book* when I realized that *that* was what I was really writing about: story, narrative, the accumulation of detail and color, the human back-and-forth we use to help us describe the journeys we're on, getting a chance at seeing who or what we might be while we're at it. Fixing up the sentences.

Are we telling the truth? Can we ever, as the famous line goes, tell the truth, the whole truth, and nothing but the truth? It's not likely. Once upon a time an immigrant Pole in his teens, trained as a blacksmith, arrived in America. Arrived with the twentieth century. He worked for many years in a Detroit foundry, moonlighted as a butcher, made and sold sausage, saved some money. Then in 1927 he bought a northern Michigan farm. One hundred and eighty pretty acres. He'd also married and fathered eleven children, nine of whom reached maturity. He continued to work hard—especially during the Great Depression—and died one morning in his apple orchard clutching a book to his chest. His wife Nelly, a pious woman of good heart, slipped that book under his arm just before Mr. Savage, the undertaker, closed the coffin. That book was the beginning of his—our—story.

Weave back. To the summers after World War II when I followed this man around his farm. I was a city kid from Flint now, but I didn't feel like one. Not completely. I was born only twenty miles north of the Szostak farm, in West Branch, a county seat town where my father had also been born and where Gramps Gildner owned a lumberyard. My parents and I in fact lived in the lumberyard until I started school, in an apartment Gramps finished off on the second floor; previously we lived in an apartment building that burned to the ground my first winter, still sleeping in a crib. Those early years in Flint, I was always eager to return up north, especially to a farm I had no trouble remembering, and now could stay at for weeks, or longer, instead of an afternoon: searching out wild blueberries in the forest, squirting milk from Princess or Bossy into a pail, collecting eggs, feeding slops to the pigs, hay to the horses.

I loved watching Grandpa Szostak take those big Belgians, Nelly and Prince, down to the creek for a drink. He would go in with them, boots and all, and, like them, drink from the stream. He'd remove his shirt and wash the day's dirt off his scarred neck, shoulders, and back—off those splotches of pink that my mother had told me came from his being burned "in that awful foundry." I didn't think they looked like scars at all; they could have been flowers pressed into his skin.

Finished washing, my grandfather would fling his arms over the shoulders of that chestnut-shiny team, smiling and renewed. Although he was in his sixties, near the end of his life, to me my grandfather, exactly like those two high-standing companions, seemed of no age; he was a force, a collection of motion and silences and sudden bursts of sound that, were I smart enough then, I would have recognized as a special kind of music.

In the middle of the day he might drop his pitchfork and go sit in the apple orchard, just sit there in the high timothy at its edge and gaze at the sky. For a length of time that, to an active boy, was simply extraordinary. I'd climb a tree and watch him, wondering: What is he looking at? What does he see? And hold myself still, waiting and waiting for clues, and finally bite into the Northern Spy I was holding, which was still too green.

One time he had Nelly and Prince hitched to a wagon and waved me over. He pulled me up to the seat, between his knees, and gave me the reins to hold. Off we went, to the field from which hay had recently been harvested. There, his hands over mine to show me how, we slapped the reins on the horses' backs just enough to pick up speed, and a little more, calling *gee!* and *haw!* until Grandma appeared, flowing toward us. Shouting in Polish, raising her fist, she certainly seemed excited. His hands still over mine, he helped me steer the wagon around and around her, her face turning redder and redder, the Polish flying faster, a fine gold shower of hay dust falling, and my grandfather singing those sounds of recklessness and affection, that operatic dip and rise of murmur and huzza—to Grandma, to me, to the magnificent team (look at them! his proud arm proclaimed)—all of which I can still see and hear when I am happy.

It never occurred to me that she might be truly angry at her husband, afraid I would be hurt. I thought, in all the drama, that this was something they did now and then.

Evenings after chores, Grandma set out platters and bowls of food gathered fresh from the farm—baked chicken, ham or sausages from Grandpa's smokehouse, great slices of beefsteak tomatoes, mashed potatoes, dill pickles, pickled beets, corn on the cob, rhubarb pie, apple pie—all prepared without electricity or hot running water. She cooked on and baked in a wood-burning stove. Her kitchen was large; her table was large. Their last child, Aunt Rita, was in high school then, as was my cousin Donny whom my grandparents took in and raised while Aunt Mary, his mother, made her long way back from depression in Traverse City, living in what was then called a *mental hospital*. Joining this foursome every summer over the years was a medley of city cousins; during my tenure I arrived with Ray, Leonard's younger brother, sons of Aunt Helen. My age and one of the toughest guys I've ever known, Ray lasted barely a week. He pined for Detroit and especially his neighborhood swimming pool where bloodsuckers did not lurk. The first day he jumped into Grandpa's creek he found one between his toes—his Achilles heel—and never went back. Farm life, he said, was for crap.

After supper, Steve knelt beside his chair and said his rosary. He returned to the chair and poured himself a shot of whiskey. Then—an astonishing thing to me—he took up a book, often producing it from inside his shirt. He was the only man in my family I ever saw read a book. I come from farmers, lumbermen, carpenters—men who, when they want the truth about something, lay a level on it and follow the bubble.

The summer I would turn eleven, I decided to stay in Flint and join a baseball team with my buddies. That was the summer Steve's heart stopped. The funeral, as it happened, was on my birthday.

It was late August, hot and humid. I had to wear my good suit, a wool navy blue, and a tie. His house was full of relatives, friends, and neighbors, ruddy-faced farmers with razor nicks, missing fingers; flowers, food, the scents of whiskey and pipe tobacco mingled with embraces and exclamations.

My grandfather lay in a coffin in the parlor and did not look like the man who had taken me for a wild ride over the shorn hayfield, not like the man who, when the black bull got loose and came into Grandma's chicken yard, locked his arm around the bull's neck and brought it to its knees, their foreheads pressed together, both of them breathing hard like two fighters who have had enough but still can't quit. The figure in the satiny box was rouged, his mustache trimmed so tidy it might have been a perfect caterpillar on his lip. I didn't like any of it. I slipped away, down to the creek, where I took off my heavy suit. I whinnied like a horse, threw stones, jumped in the water.

Almost two decades later I was visiting with Grandma in her kitchen, eating coffee cake fresh from her wood-burning stove. She had refused to leave the farm, she could manage. Uncle Joe, who lived with his family in Standish, twenty minutes away, kept the main eye on her, while her children in Flint and Detroit made regular trips to do their share. I told Grandma I had recently quit my teaching job in the Upper Peninsula and was taking a new one in Iowa. I had a car full of books and a long drive ahead. The mention of books reminded her of Grandpa's reading, that astonishing nightly event at this same oilcloth-covered table, which I hadn't given much thought to over the years. Was that possible? Quite possible. I was busy living my own story.

"Oh, yes," she said, "always reading. And always," she added, "this Korzeniowski. Always. But why?" She did not understand why.

I can still recall, at hearing Joseph Conrad's Polish name, how my neck got hot. How my hands wanted to touch that book she said she found in her dead husband's arms. Then she told me what she did with it. I reckoned, going back, that her romantic act of keeping Grandpa and his book together occurred while I was in his creek, maybe at the exact moment I was venting like a stallion, cooling off.

"Why?" my grandmother asked again, about this Korzeniowski.

Well, I wanted to know why, too. That is, I wanted to know *more*. Steve Szostak, blacksmith and farmer, a man my aunt Rita said left school after the fourth grade, was being given—his story was being given—a new, large detail. A bubble wanting to burst.

"A man's real life," Conrad wrote, "is that accorded to him in the thoughts of other men by reason of respect or natural love." I respected my grandfather, but did I love him? Or did I love the images I carried? Of a man standing in his dark smithy on the farm, his face the color of rhubarb, sending up sparks from the white-hot forge? A man searching the sky from the edge of his orchard, opening his book in the honeyed glow of a kerosene lamp at a table we all moved away from?

There are nights I wake up hearing Conrad's challenge: "The dead can live only with the exact intensity and quality of life imparted to them by the living."

I don't believe we ever exchanged a single word, my grandfather and I, because he spoke—or chose to speak—only Polish, a language I did not know as a boy. Yet we communicated—by facial expressions, pointing, a tone of voice. Now we had even more to say to each other—through Joseph Conrad's stories.

WHERE TO START? I TALKED with his three surviving children: Aunt Nettie, one of the oldest; my mother, a middle child; and Aunt Rita, the last born, who came to my grandparents after a nine-year interval when Steve was forty-eight, Nelly forty-four. Often I would ask these women the same question and receive three almost completely different answers. Not a surprise. But sometimes I'd get, without hesitation, the same response, as when I asked where and when their parents got married.

"Saint Hedwig's Church in Detroit," they said. "In 1902."

I called Saint Hedwig's to see what else I might learn. I learned that Saint Hedwig's did not open its doors until 1903. "We have no record of this marriage," a secretary assured me.

How could these three sisters be so wrong about *this* particular detail? My mother, a romantic for whom facts are usually more like suggestions anyway—as in recipes that need a little more this or that—only shrugged when I told her. Rita, who had been salutatorian of her high school class, was deeply puzzled. Nettie just said, "Life is funny, isn't it?"

Steve, I was hearing more and more, loved to tell stories about Poland's kings and queens, her musicians and poets and fabled mounted cavalry. Almost everyone said so—Aunt Rita, my mother, their youngest brother Johnny ("a teenager, a baby!" my mother cried), who, when he turned twenty, married a war widow with a young daughter and was almost immediately overseas fighting in World War II. (The family's oldest son, Stanley, performed a quicker leap to see action: he managed, at fourteen, to get into World War I and to stay in for six months, gaining a magnificent portrait of himself in dress uniform, including the grand campaign hat, until his grandmother, Nelly's mother, mounted a full frontal attack upon the army and got him out, because Steve would do nothing about it, nor allow Grandma to do anything, saying the boy should learn something.)

Late into the night, with a good audience, my grandfather could go on and on. "Even my wife Marge, who didn't understand a word of Polish, was crazy about Steve's stories," Leonard told me. "Because he seemed to *be* the story, if you know what I mean." And Queen Jadwiga, a famous beauty, very generous and smart—the architect of Kraków who built the cathedral, improved the great Jagiellonian University, contributed her jewels to help pay for such things, and much more—was one of Steve's favorites.

Jadwiga and Hedwig are the same woman. All those years in Detroit, the family lived only a short walk from Saint Hedwig's Church, faithfully attended Mass, and Steve and Nelly sent their kids to Saint Hedwig's School. Could it be that Nettie, Jean, and Rita were so taken by their father's stories about the splendid Jadwiga that they couldn't imagine a better-named church for him to wed their mother in? Perhaps, caught up in his storytelling, he even insinuated as much? In any case, although the sisters were factually wrong about the church, they were close enough to the heart of the matter to feel its heat and beat.

Pursuing this man, I knew what I did not want—an accumulation of fleshless facts, the exact number of clacking bones in a skeleton. I wanted what Joseph Conrad wanted—the questions, the mysteries, the imperfections and contradictions of the human heart.

At one point about four years into the writing of *My Grandfather's Book*, when I had accumulated more mystery and imperfection than I thought I could handle, I was visiting my mother in Flint. (Actually next door to Flint, in the outskirts of the little town of Grand Blanc, where my father built the dream house she wanted; but no one in my family said we lived in Grand Blanc, I think because it had a slightly snooty reputation—the Buick Open golf tournament was held there, for example—and, besides, we went to school and church and shopped in Flint.) We were sitting in my mother's back yard, splitting a beer, the autumn-hazy day easing away. I fell to musing about the large photograph of Grandma that hung in my mother's house and which I wanted to make a copy of. Nelly is sixteen in the picture, wearing a rose in her hair; soon she will marry my grandfather.

Here I go again, seeing Nelly's portrait hanging on my parents' bedroom wall, then on only my mother's bedroom wall after my father died. I see these two women facing each other, finally, after spending the late afternoon in their gardens, alone, thinking how lovely everything is, how temporary . . .

Suddenly my mother said, "Why are you doing this, Gary?"

"Doing what?" I said.

"Asking all these questions, collecting all this stuff. We're nobody—nobodies—never done anything except work hard and die. Why don't you leave us be!"

I might have quoted Yeats to her: "What can I but enumerate old themes?" Or Borges: "Life is too poor not to be also immortal." I might have brought up Conrad's Lord Jim, who errs and errs and errs again trying to achieve grace, salvation. But I was off-balance ("leave *us* be"?), almost on my knees among the red and yellow leaves in her yard.

Well, maybe she was right.

When I got back to my desk I decided to pursue a short story notion I'd made a few notes about, to take my mind off my family, to leave them be. I liked the tentative title, "The Rug-Beater of Żoliborz."

Żoliborz was the section of Warsaw where I had lived during 1987-88 when I was a Fulbright professor and Poland was still behind the Iron Curtain. On Saturday mornings I often stood at my window watching a white-haired man across the street clean his rugs, beating dust from the flowers and birds and sailing vessels woven into them. He was coming back to me, and all over again he seemed not to be knocking dust into the air so much as releasing color and scent and song, revealing to that oppressed and cheerless country a way of escape. If I could describe this well enough, it might lead me to the next thing and the next, and I could leave my family alone. The only problem was, the old man of Żoliborz was turning out in my story to look like my grandfather. He wouldn't leave *me* alone.

Why? Because he delighted and puzzled and engaged me. Challenged me. Because he strode into his creek and helped himself to a drink like a horse. Sat in his orchard and gazed for who knows how long at the sky? Took me for a wild wagon ride, exercising my fist-shaking sweet old grandmother—whose wedding ring he once cut off her bee-stung, swollen hand while she, fearing God-knew-what-cataclysm a broken band might release, pleaded with him not to do it. Because he stood in a soaking rage cursing the heavens for the hail ruining his crops. I knew no one like him.

"What's the hardest thing in the world to do?" my father once asked me.

I had in mind, I remember, an answer related to construction, for at that moment he was building a house for my dog. I was handing him the nails, thinking.

He said, "I'll tell you. Getting from here to there."

"To where?"

"To wherever you're going," he said.

It seemed to me, years later, that my father paused and regarded me as if he suddenly realized something—realized that when we finished nailing together those boards we knelt among in our backyard, finished building the doghouse, that I would soon be starting to pack my bag, knot my tie, take his hand and say, "I'll be seeing you."

It seemed to me—if such a thought, about the swiftness of time, was contained in his look—that I left home before either of us would, or could, have predicted. Not after high school when I was expected to go, but those summers I went to the farm—when, delivered to my grandfather, I began to feel, and thrill to, a sense of separateness. We sat in the same apple orchard, stepped around the same cow flop, used the same bootjack, the same creek, same stars, smelled the same dusk, and heard the same killdeer shriek its final evening song.

But taking in those things together did not make me feel close to him, connected to another, in a way I was used to. They made me feel closer to myself, to my own ears and eyes and the shadows and bright figures inside my head I wanted to follow.

ONE NIGHT, THINKING ABOUT STEVE Szostak and Joseph Conrad, I bleated out to myself, "Look at all they had in common!" Both were adolescents in the Austrian-occupied part of Poland and fled the country as teenagers. Both were sixty-six when they died—in English-speaking countries—in August—of heart attacks. Their birthdays were within a week of each other (Steve's on November 27, Conrad's on December 3); both were Sagittarians, born under the sign of the Archer. (I even looked in that day's newspaper for their horoscope reading: "Tempers may flare, but at least the conflict is out in the open.") Both men had famous tempers. Each one named his last son John (Steve named his next-to-last Joseph) and each man, late in life, created a woman named Rita: my grandfather literally, Conrad in literature—Rita de Lastaola, a peasant girl who finds great riches and the virtuous gun-running George in *The Arrow of Gold*, a lesser novel written in 1919 when Conrad was sixty-two, his powers waning. At sixty-two, my grandfather one day was standing beside Rita when one of his daughters-in-law snapped their picture and caught him looking puzzled.

Both men were dreamers—their biggest connection, as I see it. In their forties they abandoned large industrial cities to live in the country. Conrad left London for Pent Farm (but to husband his memories and sentences, not the soil) and Steve Szostak left Detroit for land he didn't intend to farm that hard. My grandfather bought his pretty place (rolling fields surrounded by forest, a stream running through) in that heady year 1927 when an airmail pilot called Slim Lindbergh, another dreamer, soloed the Atlantic, the stock market was soaring, and Babe Ruth walloped an astronomical sixty homeruns. Why couldn't a blacksmith who had put some money together dream of being a gentleman farmer? He could for a little while; then the Great Depression came round the bend. Joseph Conrad and my grandfather both chose wives who provided domestic comfort and stability—Jessie and Nelly—efficient women who were not readers and who learned to stand back when the brooding began.

"How little I really knew of the man I married," said one.

"I didn't always understand my husband," said the other.

RECORDS. DATES. NAMES ON PAPER and in stone and in the watery memories we carry and often care for beyond reason . . . and they mean less and less; they become less and less, as the various winds come and go, harsh and sweet, in their seasons.

Or they mean more, become much more, but how do we grasp it, that increase? That newness or strangeness? How do we recognize it, hold it?

During the Great Depression, the war, those years of too little and too much and of harboring hard thoughts that matter, my grandfather put seed in the earth and milked his cows. He watched the sky as farmers have always watched the sky, and believers, too, romantics, scientists, and those who fear, carry doubt. He thought, surely, of Ostrów, that long-ago village he had left, and of youth, his brothers, the journey to America, his wife and children. He grieved over the loss of Karol, his first born, who lived only three days, and of losing Stella, a young teenager, to the great flu epidemic. But surely he was thankful to see his sons Joe and Johnny come home from the war, for the most part intact, though Johnny would carry shrapnel in his head and legs for the rest of his life; and thankful, surely, for Rita, that sunny late gift, and for Nelly, no longer sad at leaving Detroit, where he'd been hurt in Henry Ford's foundry. When they brought him home, my mother crawled under the kitchen table, she remembered, and Grandma was unable to stop making the sign of the cross. She recalled especially the long heavy silence that came over Grandma, who for many days would make her way up the street to kneel almost prone in a pew, seeking further absolution for the loss of Karol and Stella, never forgotten, and now for almost losing her husband. (". . . an astonishingly vital people," the poet Czesław Miłosz says of the Slavs, "who sink easily into moronic apathy. . .")

Perhaps those summers when I watched my grandfather gaze at the sky from his orchard or bend his burning face to the water, perhaps those summers when I witnessed his impotent fist raised at the hail, that falling-to-his-knees embrace with the black bull that nothing it seemed could separate, perhaps in those seasons named sweet and harsh he was taken by all of it, them, continuance and silence, those two unwavering blooms in the fields beyond—but taken where, exactly?

ON NOVEMBER 28, 1927—NELLY'S BIRTHDAY—MY grandfather
is riding in a truck piled high with those things most of us collect,
leaving Detroit for this farm he has bought. What are his
thoughts? That today his wife is forty-one? That yesterday he
turned forty-five? That 1927 is their silver anniversary? It's
also the silver anniversary of Charles A. Lindbergh's birth in
Detroit and the invention of the Animal Crackers box, which is
designed to look like a car in a P. T. Barnum circus train; but I
doubt these last two anniversaries are among Steve's thoughts
as much as they are among mine.

My grandfather is more likely to be thinking that in twenty-
five years he and Nelly have produced ten children, eight of
whom are living, and half of that number—those still in the
nest—are riding in the car up ahead with their mother. That
thirty years ago he left his father's farm in Ostrów in what
should have been Polonia but for the thieving Austrians. He left
with the clothes on his back and a loaf of bread and since that
time has been wanting to return and is now returning. According
to the rhythms and fiery figures of his thought, he has served
his penance in the noisy graceless world, in burning purgatory,
received his scars, and now is going back, as close as he can, to
whence he came.

Before it's too late. Before his eyes, like the weary eyes of
the man of finance, the man of accounts, and the man of law—
those men in Conrad's story "Youth" who are listening to
Marlow's tale of the *Judea* and her wretched 600-ton cargo of
burning coal which is trying to reach Bangkok—before his eyes,
like theirs, fall to "looking still, looking always, looking anxiously
for something out of life, that while it is expected is already
gone—has passed unseen, in a sigh, in a flash—together with
the youth, with the strength, with the romance of illusions."

Monday, November 28, 1927, is a fact. So are the inventions
"Youth" and the Animal Crackers box (and the lions and giraffes

that children find inside and are pleased to nibble on), and P. T. Barnum and the caravan taking a Polish-American family from the Motor City to a farm 150 miles straight north. A farm that my mother, seeing it, thought was "gray, gray, gray, and muddy everywhere." At eleven she was old enough to have seen up close Grand Circus Park in neon-bright, roaring twenties downtown Detroit, and she had not wanted to leave it. Nor did she want to leave a regular event she had either been slow to tell me about or did mention and I hadn't been ready to receive it, i.e. the trolley Steve gave her the pennies to ride to the public library on Woodward Avenue with the note she was to show the lady behind the desk for the books he wanted. Nor did my mother want to leave the treat she could buy with the penny left over, which she ate in front of the recently built Fillmore or Senate theatres, in whose richly colored posters she could see the beautiful Greta Garbo and Gloria Swanson and Joan Crawford; and the even more fabulous Fox Theatre was coming soon! These are some spectacular facts informing her description of a gray farm whose approach was through mud—in the end an altogether disappointing, gritty-slick trail of raw facts presented to me reluctantly, I think; still, there they are, doing their best to hang on.

As the fact of Prohibition is doing its best to hang on, and the facts of Detroit's notorious extortionists the Purple Gang, F. Scott Fitzgerald's novel *This Side of Paradise*, and the great Polish poet Adam Mickiewicz's skull wrapped in its special tomb. But the thoughts, dreams, desires, or even prayers of my grandfather on November 28, 1927, or on any other day, can no more be measured or weighed than the *Judea*, or the island of Patusan where Lord Jim ends up, or the Black man's blood in *Heart of Darkness* that fills Marlow's shoes, and I know it.

I know that Steve Szostak, water and bone, could have been measured and weighed and probably was; I know I could take a shovel and dig him out and lay him on a scale—the same as with a book by Joseph Conrad or Emily Dickinson or Shakespeare. But something beyond these facts will be elusive. I can feel it, this slippery thing, feel its light, passion, confusion, or mystery until I shake, sing, swoon, or go mad. But I can't measure it, can't lay a level across it to find the bubble perfectly centered, and I know it.

The facts and memories of our lives—how they can hound us into chasing after them, that we might keep up with them, catch them, shape them into a visible, composed, embraceable thing.

Thanks to Information, of all sources, I found in Chicago a man named Stanley Szostak, the 14th and last child of Steve's brother Pete; and thanks to Stanley Szostak, who found it in a box of things his wife put together before she died, I received in the mail one day Steve and Nelly's formal wedding portrait. For at least a decade I had been wondering if such a picture existed, and now here it was, arriving, I fancied, like one of those small birds that flies off a telephone line and goes somewhere else for a change.

My grandfather looks at me from 1902 ready for anything— marriage, kids, hard work, success, America. He has a rose fixed to his coat, a cigar between his fingers, and beside him his young bride, a Polish-American girl who puts a hand on his arm and keeps it there, no matter what, for forty-seven years; and then just before Mr. Savage closes the coffin, she gives him for company a book about the passions and mysteries of the heart, a book about two foreigners making their separate ways in the jungle, one of whom is trying to understand the other.

Is there a better story to help me on my journey?

Street-Smart

When my daughter Gretchen and her son Gabriel, a toddler, came to visit me in Poland the summer of 1988, a Pole who couldn't win a place on the baseball team I was coaching, the Sparks, won one in my daughter's heart. For three weeks in Warsaw, followed by many letters and recorded outpourings on tape carried over the Atlantic by Lot, the Polish airlines, Jacek Demkiewicz courted my romantic daughter like a man trying to stay alive. He courted her in the Old World by telling her the romantic stories that Poles have been telling each other, their children, and beyond for as long as their country has existed and struggled and suffered under occupation and survived in the sun to say her poems and play her music again; and he showed Gretchen the places where many of those poets, composers, artists, and other makers of the heart's language paused in their journeys to sup or sleep and where they finally lay down from their labors to rest forever, under fresh flowers delivered daily by grateful countrymen. To remind all lovers that romance still lived.

Jacek Demkiewicz showed my daughter where Frédéric François Chopin's literal heart had come home to repose in glory in Warsaw's Church of the Holy Cross (while his body lay in the soil of Paris's Père Lachaise cemetery), and he showed her the statue of Poland's great national poet Adam Mickiewicz, in whose tall shadow couples might kiss, believing that this buss would bring them even closer, as nothing else could. Jacek Demkiewicz was tall, fast afoot, a good soccer player, though not supple enough to use his entire body in concert with a bat or a small hard white ball; he especially did not possess what baseball players call "soft hands." A baseball will bounce off hard hands, as it will off wood; but soft hands cradle the ball, give it a nest. Jacek's truest talent may well have been his ability to slip around the Communist system to get things that most Poles could not get—or not get as easily. Jacek was street-smart and proud of it. He was friends with the Sparks' founder and general manager, Darius Luszczyna, a former journalist, who employed Jacek to get us things.

Jacek had taught himself pretty good American English— perhaps his second truest talent—in large part by listening closely to and mimicking song lyrics on hard-to-get American CDs. He could get them. His dream was to manage a fabulously famous band, something like the Beatles, only specializing in heavy metal. He knew heavy metal like the back—and front—of his hands. At one time he was a disk jockey on Polish radio, but something happened. He had gone too far. Too far doing what, exactly, was never spelled out. It was enough for Jacek to make a face of disgust and say, simply, "The Communists." To his fellow Poles, including Dariusz and the players, this explained why he was no longer a DJ, as it explained everything else in their world that carried forth frustration, failure, drunkenness, grief, empty store shelves, and in many cases a sudden early violent death.

After Gretchen and Gabe returned to the States for her to resume her studies at Drake University, I stayed in Poland to finish out the baseball season. Drake, where I was on the faculty, had granted me a sabbatical for the coming academic year, thus I did not have to rush back—having wrapped up my Fulbright duties teaching American lit at the University of Warsaw, my official reason for being in Poland during 1987 and 1988. I had applied for the sabbatical, from Warsaw, because I was eligible for one and because I had started writing *The Warsaw Sparks* and wanted to focus on it. Which developed—receiving my sabbatical, that is—into the kind of milk-and-water entertainment that can happen in academia.

After the list of grantees was published on campus, a friend in the English department told me that some of my colleagues became very unhappy. How can Gildner receive a sabbatical when he hasn't been here like the rest of us! It wasn't right! Their unhappiness was transported—as if by a mule-drawn caisson draped in funeral black, one imagined—to the first meeting of the liberal arts faculty following the announcement of sabbatical recipients. A motion was actually made and seconded, my friend reported, to amend the faculty handbook so that nothing like what Gildner did could ever happen again.

It happened because, back when student enrollment in the nation's private colleges and universities had fallen off, the Drake administration saw a real benefit to granting leaves at no pay to faculty members who were invited to teach elsewhere as visiting professors. Such leaves of course brought relief to Drake's bottom line and did not affect sabbatical eligibility. Theoretically, I could have been on leave for six years, teaching at other institutions or not teaching if I could afford it, and the seventh year I would be eligible for a paid sabbatical from Drake. I came close to doing exactly that, which is what caused such unhappiness among some of my stay-at-home colleagues. In any event, the motion to right this wrong, I was told, passed. I never bothered to look it up, myself. To find that balm had not been applied to such unhappiness, after all, would have been too sad and, besides, snuffed my story.

I arrived back in the States only minutes, it seemed, before the Berlin Wall came down, so I did not get to see in person the surely complex expressions of disbelief and joy on the faces of my Polish friends. The Soviet bear had finally—a miracle!—rolled over, perhaps in a fetal position, and commenced to suck its paw. Jacek Demkiewicz was frantic to leave Poland—specifically for the USA. He had great plans. Which of course included Gretchen. She, almost daily, appealed to me for help. Jacek needed an invitation from someone in America—someone whose invitation our embassy in Warsaw would pay attention to when Jacek brought it there in his gladdest hand, his other holding a packed suitcase, ready, man, to go.

Almost a century earlier, sixteen-year-old Stefan Szostak was ready to go, too; but not because a foreign bully suddenly lost its chokehold on Stefan's native land. Quite the opposite. Young Stefan's Poland, during a bleak time called Partition, did not in political fact exist—only her geographical shape existed, if you looked past the hacking that had divided her into three more or less equal parts, taken and occupied, respectively, by Russia, Prussia, and Austria. Underscoring Stefan's feeling of suffocation, his birth certificate declared that he was one of those thieves, an Austrian, which may well be why he spoke only Polish or nothing his three score and seven years.

Stefan Szostak carried no letter of invitation. My future grandfather's most important possession as he made his way— even more important than his loaf of bread—was a language made very difficult, the Poles insisted, because it was their one valuable that no one could easily steal, followed by, for merely practical reasons, the shoes on his feet. He did have one large thing in common with Jacek Demkiewicz: as a trained blacksmith he, too, was knowledgeable about heavy metal.

I TOLD GRETCHEN I WOULD BE happy to write a letter to the American embassy in Warsaw supporting Jacek's quest for a visa as soon as she finished all her course work at Drake. I explained why. She protested that she would *not* be distracted by Jacek's presence.

"You may believe that," I said, "but distraction will happen."

"It won't."

"Do only I discern the pain of hearts that yearn?"

"Now really, Dad."

"As soon as you finish your last exam."

"That's next year!"

"Next year—and your last semester—begins in a couple of months."

"Jacek is dying."

"He is only in love. His chances of surviving are at least fifty-fifty."

Let me back up a moment. After high school, Gretchen entered Hamline University in Minnesota. She left at mid-year to go on an adventure. Gabe became part of it, born in a Nicaraguan barrio in Florida. When she realized she was not where she wanted to be, the Nicaraguans said fine, she could go, but the baby would stay. She went to New York, got a job in a Manhattan day care, was soon helping to manage it. One day, with her friend Maura, she flew to Miami; and while Maura waited in a rented car down the street, Gretchen spoke to Gabe's sitter—a Nicaraguan teenager she knew who was minding a house full of small children—convincing the girl she was only in town briefly, on business, and only wanted to take Gabe for a little walk. Thus my tall, rangy, romantic daughter, whose natural goodness and cheerful outlook have kept her among the happiest people I know, got her son back.

Not long after what might be called Gretchen's street-smart caper, she and Gabe moved to Des Moines to live with me in her childhood home and, at Drake, resume pursuing a college degree.

The fall semester following her trip to Poland, Gretchen's academic performance was splendid, and she all but said to me: see, I *am* serious about school. She also continued to lobby for Jacek. So after she registered for a full load of classes in the spring, though I knew in my bones something not good would come from it, I wrote the letter inviting Jacek Demkiewicz to Des Moines, Iowa, where I said he would visit and be a good boy, I believed, and not steal a US citizen's job.

Why didn't I wait? Because, as a writer, I am always on the lookout for conflict? No. Because I have an appetite for the raw meat of masochism? I actually prefer seafood, greens, and pasta. Because I love my daughter with whom I share perhaps too much romantic DNA and want to make her happy? Yes. Did I soon regret writing and mailing that letter? Yes.

Jacek got his visa and arrived in the Hawkeye State ready to show his best moves. Plan A on his list pointed straight at New York City and the chiefs of the music industry to whom he would pitch his famous band idea. He would not bother with letters or phone calls: in person, man to man, was his style in Warsaw (leave the stupid Communists out of it) and since New York City, he said, was the Warsaw of America and he was a big city boy—street-smart—he would make out fine. No one could advise him in this matter, though some tried.

"Jacek, New York doesn't know who you are."

"I will tell them."

"Jacek, you don't have anything to show."

"I will tell them."

"Jacek, you will be lucky to meet the people who guard the doors—"

"I will tell them."

SO JACEK DEMKIEWICZ BOUNDED ABOARD a Greyhound bus for the Big Apple in his best shirt, Air Jordan knockoffs, and biggest, most confident smile; and while he was there, smitten by the famous lights and sights like many a tourist but mainly trying to tell someone important his dream of leading heavy metal to shining glory, he spent all the money he had set aside for this trip, plus much more, and spoke to no one in an office who was important, except one time to a receptionist—anyway, he supposed that's what she was, she dressed nice—and then he came back to Iowa looking stunned and thinner.

Gretchen and Gabe had moved from my house to an apartment; it was just roomy enough for them and for Gabe's lab-retriever mix, Brahms, and now for Jacek, and when I saw my daughter she was looking a little stunned, too. She was also dropping courses and adding yet another part-time job to contribute, she said, to the family. I couldn't bear to ask what she meant by "the family"; I could only guess that Jacek, with her help, was working on Plan B—his US citizenship.

They had a small, quiet wedding. I learned about it a week or so later. Gretchen's graduation from Drake that spring and *then* her reunion with Jacek—my preferred scenario—did not happen. The roof on my house was wanting to fall in, as well, creating both a painful symbolism and, come rain and snow, a possible slough over the area where I usually sat quietly and tried to write. The roofer I hired tore off five or six layers of old shingles (a major cause of the imminent caving in) and put on a new roof but then drove away leaving all the old shingles scattered over my lawn where I used to play catch with my grandson. And once upon a time with Gretchen, for whom I wrote "Playing Catch With My Daughter"—

> I remember the walnuts
> uncurling, the lilacs on call,
> the day's sweet revolution
> and verdurous smell.
> I had just cut the grass.
> And yes,
> when she kicked out

and followed through
all that green day,
how the little spears flew.

ON THE PLUS SIDE, *THE Warsaw Sparks* had come out and, after I was interviewed about it by Bob Edwards on NPR's *Morning Edition*, the English department secretary told me she counted 15 movie producers trying to reach me to talk about the film rights. Most of these producers, it turned out, wanted to make a comedy—another *Bad News Bears*, Polish style—and I was not interested. *The Warsaw Sparks* does have humor—a story about Polish guys playing a game they didn't grow up with has plenty of goofy moments; but there is more to the story— i.e., *Polish Life*, the phrase my players often used to summarize their frustrations in simply getting from here to there.

Which helped to explain why they loved baseball: it was precise, American, and it allowed them to get home, where, under Communism, they were not. The getting home part—on the field and in the heart—is something many Americans, especially if they love baseball, readily understand. The producer who said he, too, was the grandson of an immigrant and understood the book's metaphor of "getting home" promised if he got the film rights he would be faithful to that metaphor. He also thought the movie should be in black and white, and shot in Poland.

I sold him the film rights. My granddaughter Joanna was born. I held her. Gretchen and I hugged, and I helped her go back to Drake and finish that last semester. Wearing his Air Jordan knockoffs, the laces untied and dragging the ground, according to current teenage fashion, Jacek helped me load all those shingles in my yard on a truck and haul them off to the dump.

Also on the plus side, Jacek was good with Gabe, giving him lessons in soccer. He was good, as well, with Gretchen—or as good as he could be. He didn't get far in showing America his best street-smart moves and had trouble understanding why he wasn't succeeding; but he didn't get so frustrated as to take out his failures on his wife. She, for her part, got the picture fairly quickly and would soon be saying to him that she had three children to look after, not two.

Like many growing up under Communism, Jacek had latched on to some honeyed fantasies so hard that his development had been arrested in special ways. One of those ways—which we in the West contributed to—called for, at times demanded, a vision of the free world as a near-perfect place, especially America, where the citizens, Jacek and his fellow dreamers needed to believe, drove sleek new cars, wore the latest fashions, and speared their thick T-bones with golden forks. (I exaggerate about the forks.) My students at the University of Warsaw—who were smart—hated the novel *Fat City* I assigned them. They did not want to believe that its main character, Billy Tully, an on-the-skids white prize fighter in California—in sunny California, of all places, home of Hollywood!—was reduced to working in the fields like a migrant, breaking his back for a measly few dollars in order to buy his jug of cheap vino. Not this handsome virile boxer! Not in America!

After Gretchen got her BA, she and Jacek and the children moved to Iowa City and the University of Iowa so she could pursue graduate work and, as insurance, certification to teach high school English. It was in Iowa City where Gretchen and Jacek parted amicably. He moved to Minneapolis and found a job at Best Buy in its music department. Gretchen did well at the university and received several good offers to teach, including one from Houston, Texas, that was astonishingly generous. I did not want her and the children to live in the hot, humid cement sprawl of Houston, but I kept my mouth shut. Finally she accepted an offer from Delhi High School in rural northeast Iowa and bought a house with a big, leafy back yard in nearby Manchester, not far from Dubuque—and not all that far from Minneapolis, making it easy for Jacek to see his daughter and kick the soccer ball around with Gabe.

In the midst of all this, a number of notable things happened. Drake's Center for the Humanities, on my recommendation, brought to campus from Gdańsk, Poland, Jacek and Anna Mydlarski. Anna, a Solidarity worker from its beginning, had helped produce a BBC documentary about the history of that great movement and its role in the headaches the Poles constantly gave the Soviet Union. She had translated several of my poems into Polish (translation was one of her professions), arranged for me to participate in underground readings that were strictly forbidden by the Communist government, and brought me to meet Lech Wałęsa. Jacek was an important young painter in Poland. As scholar- and artist-in-residence, respectively, they gave public lectures and presentations at Drake and at venues from Omaha to Chicago during the year they lived in Des Moines. They brought along their young son and daughter and enrolled them in public school, where they performed beautifully, and we all had a wonderful time.

Down at the Polk County Court House in Des Moines, to help things from becoming too wonderful, I was being sued for alimony by an American teacher who claimed that we had had a common law marriage in Poland. A trial was held, lasting three days, and the judge found that there had been no marriage—that my invitation to Vicki to join me in Warsaw, and her acceptance, was no more than that. The good parts of this story are all in *The Warsaw Sparks.* Many years later, at Gretchen's wedding to Brian Robinson, I was pleased to see

Vicki again and learn that she had been recently named Iowa Teacher of the Year.

The world does turn and yearn. I got married again—ten years after Gretchen's mother and I divorced. I married Elizabeth, a part-time graphics designer at *Better Homes and Gardens.* Davidson College in North Carolina invited me down there to occupy an endowed chair as writer-in-residence for two semesters; since Gretchen was pointed in a good direction and the Mydlarskis were back in Gdańsk with some money in their pockets, I was glad to accept.

The movie producer I had signed up with phoned almost weekly. Robin Williams, heavily committed to several projects, was nonetheless very interested in playing Darius, the Sparks' general manager, and the producer and everyone else on our project were excited. HBO was interested in making a movie of the book, but my producer was not interested, nor was I. Kevin Costner read the script, liked the role of the American coach, and was giving *The Sparks* serious thought, then finally passed—having just starred in *Bull Durham* (the best film about baseball, many believe, including me), he wanted to try other subjects. Kevin Bacon read the script and wanted to play the American coach—which I was in favor of—but the producer didn't think Bacon was A-list enough to raise the money they needed. Robin Williams, it developed, could not find a free space among his commitments. There were many other actors who expressed interest, plus several A-list directors, but nothing happened beyond this high-end talk during my enjoyable stay in North Carolina.

I did, however, receive another Fulbright, this time to Hungary. But the Hungarians, now able, after Communism, to make their own decisions, couldn't somehow get together regarding their part in hosting the American scholars, so I and all my fellow nominees to Hungary were in limbo.

Being in limbo, I thought, was dull. Going back to Des Moines was not all that exciting either. I decided to leave Drake. Quit, move, and devote my best hours to writing, give a few readings to feed the kitty. A Drake administrator said I didn't want to just walk away from my full professorship and tenure, I would be giving up some goodies I'd earned.

Like what? I said.

Oh, like use of the library, free parking for life, free tuition for my dependents, and health insurance. Also, Drake would pay me for my tenure. Early retirement was the way to go, he said, and worked up some papers.

Elizabeth and I drove to northern Idaho, which I had seen up close a decade earlier tooling through in an almost perfectly preserved 1946 Chevy to begin a two-year visit at Reed College in Oregon. I had tucked away Idaho's Clearwater Mountains as a good place to live, fish, and write in my later years. We gave ourselves two weeks—made a game out of it—to find the right place, if we could. On the next-to-last day we were looking at a house on a mountain with a spectacular view and a breeze in the conifers all around that called up passages of Samuel Barber's "Adagio for Strings." Elizabeth wasn't sure. It was kind of isolated, wasn't it? That was one of its best features, I thought. I also liked seeing the South Fork of the Clearwater River way down there glittering in the sun like a woman's favorite bracelet.

Next morning I learned that the Fulbright office in Washington had found another country for me— Czechoslovakia—if I wanted. I wanted. I also wanted that house on the mountain. I bought it. Then Elizabeth and I drove back to Iowa and packed for Prague. From there we took the train to Slovakia, where we would spend the next year and where Margaret, our daughter, would be conceived.

I taught American lit at Šafárika University in Prešov, an old market town whose cobbled streets went back almost 900 years. The number of inhabitants was hard to pin down; it might have been as many as 130,000 or as few as what you saw right then looking out the window. The number, always a guess, depended on whom you asked, and where, when, and how much shrug was in the shoulders.

That autumn, 1992, was gorgeous and three years, almost exactly, from when the Wall came down. We lived, Elizabeth and I, in Sečov, a residential area named for a little brook that the developers had destroyed. Our street—Dumbierska—meant something like *ginger*, and the road connecting us to downtown Prešov was called Sibirska—meaning Siberia. A bus would carry us back and forth for two crowns. Or on foot we could take a short cut through a forest where Romani lived, which I liked to do, though Elizabeth did not. The Romani kids and I had spontaneously got up a game in mime. I would pretend to be lost and they would offer to show me the way. Giggling and rolling their eyes, each child promoted a different direction. I'd try a few steps wherever a finger pointed and finally end up rolling my eyes and laughing with them.

Our building, one of many concrete-colored prefab Soviet-inspired high rises, was new. We lived on the sixth floor. Later we learned that, before Communism and Sečov, the area where we lived was called the Parsley Fields. Because that's what was there, literally meadows and meadows of it, and where people strolled on Sundays with their wicker baskets to picnic, pick wildflowers *and* parsley, and lie back in the grass with their shoes off. To say "the Parsley Fields," now—in Slavic of course— was to issue an ironic and bitter curse. Uttered even by the people who had lined up, perhaps even paid a bribe, to acquire one of the coveted flats in that bland future. The neighbors we got to know freely admitted that they were among the bribers.

"Freedom," says Krishnamurti, "is when bondage is understood."

The first time I looked out our living room window I saw the unfinished neighborhood bunker. When the revolution arrived, the workers didn't know who would pay them to complete their labor and walked away. There it lay for three years now, a basement big as a soccer field collecting rain and rats.

A small boy on a tricycle appears. I have written about him before, hoping to settle him down. But being a boy on a trike, he will not settle. He needs to ram the ugliness blocking his way, this thing full of water and rats. He rams it over and over. He can do nothing else. *We* can do nothing else.

It continues, this nightmare, developing into a sinister phantasmagoria. Watching government-orchestrated TV, we are encouraged to soften our thoughts, to dream, to travel in other directions: tall, long-limbed, gleaming young women in jewels, furs, evening gowns, motorcycle gear, and bikinis will help us, show us how much fun it is to throw back their hair, throw off care, and parade. They hold up glossy photos that hint at what *they* are dreaming of: swimming pools, cocktail lounges, the cabins of airplanes carrying fun-lovers having, well, lots of fun.

Meanwhile, the country known since 1918 as Czechoslovakia was preparing to conduct a national divorce, a split encouraged most loudly by the Slovak president, Vladimir Mečiar, a former boxer and Communist. A pretty dumb thing to do, a great many citizens said. Even the Slovaks, who had the most to lose, held up their palms. Why make such a move? Often one heard their wonderfully tuned expression *za'hada*, which covered everything they did not understand. But for Mečiar, my students told me, there was never a mystery—about anything—because he feared nothing that "came down the road." In other words, he was street-smart.

Listen—that wail again—the nightmare's old sweet song. From the usual darkness. Not to worry. He or she will soon stop.

A year or so later, back in the States, I sat at my desk on the mountain and wrote "In Development No. 3"—

> After the revolution I was standing on a balcony with my hosts when a man from above us came flying down. His shadow passed over several balconies across the way like a black ribbon, a streamer, and met him in the street. People walking to and fro gave the body plenty of room, as if it might suddenly spring upon them. Out of the silence, a siren—sounding more like someone practicing a calliope, trying, over and over, to complete a happy line. This stopped when a van arrived. White-coated attendants removed the body. Then women appeared on the balconies around us pinning up diapers and shirts, brushing their hair; men came out to smoke, resting their arms casually along the railings. One at the highest level—he wore an undershirt, a fedora—picked up a small child and they leaned over the railing together, gazing down at older children playing in the street. No voices were raised anywhere. The children, especially, seemed so quiet they might have been challenged to see who could hold his tongue the longest. I didn't know what to say myself. Finally—stupidly—I asked my hosts the name of this street. One shrugged. Another said it was the name of a distant mountain, or an herb on the mountain, she couldn't remember which. All of them agreed it was only a name, like all the other names assigned without thought to such places, and meant nothing.

THE SOUTHERN BORDER OF POLAND, by bus, was an hour or two north of Prešov. During a break in my classes, I crossed the border to find the village where Stephan Szostak was born and lived until he was sixteen. I was working on a second memoir, *My Grandfather's Book*. Had been working on it even before my

Fulbright to Poland, during which *The Warsaw Sparks* demanded to be written first.

Now I was back in Eastern Europe, in the village of my grandfather. All around me were thatched roofs shaded by modest orchards, kitchen chairs set out under the boughs of apple and cherry trees. I saw a woman and her cow at the threshold of a small shed. The woman settled on a stool. Cooing for the cow, she pressed her forehead into the animal's side and pulled at the freckled teats to put milk in her pail. I saw a horse hitched to a wooden plow. I remembered my grandfather pulling the sweat-stained harness off Prince and fondly slapping the horse's foamy hindquarters. He was a man with whom I never exchanged one word, because we did not have a language in common beyond pointing and showing. Pointing and showing worked well enough for a small boy and his grandfather, but now I wanted more from this man who had been buried on my eleventh birthday.

Just before the undertaker closed the coffin, my grandmother placed under her husband's arm the book she'd found him holding at his death. Almost two decades later, she told me when and how she gave him back his book. A book written in the language of passion. The language that Jozef Korzeniowski—Joseph Conrad—spent his life using, trying to bring people closer to the mysteries beating in the human heart. That an immigrant from a country that had been stolen read Conrad's stories in Polish only underscores *his* passion.

When my pious grandmother wanted me, as a teacher, to tell her why her husband was so attached to this Korzeniowski, I could only think to say she must read "Youth" and *Heart of Darkness* and *Lord Jim* and *Nostromo* and all the others. I also thought to ask her the title of the book she placed under his arm. I did neither. I was on my own, as was my grandfather, along with Chopin and Mozart and the kings and queens who listened to them, the servants who poured their wine, and the dreamer who wrote the book *I* place under Steve Szostak's arm. For all that it says about all of us making our way—crossing an ocean, running for home, or working the hard streets we come to.

Fact and Fiction with Konwicki

I am invited by the *Review of Contemporary Fiction* to write an essay about the Polish novelist Tadeusz Konwicki. It's beautiful autumn on the mountain and I am happy. I have a new daughter. I toss my lure over the South Fork's shimmering brown pebbles and come home with rainbows for dinner. I am even happy on my knees pulling up giant Canadian thistles that are advancing toward my new trees—the apple and plum I giddily promised, back in Budapest, to plant in the baby's honor.

But I said *yes* to the Konwicki essay and need to get ready for it. I turn my thoughts to a gray, gritty, miserable time for a lot of people—Poland under Communism, Konwicki's backdrop, headache, and—to use a fine old word in a twisted way—his muse.

It will not surprise me if personal things I do not intend to include in the essay get in anyway.

I'm writing an essay—an attempt, a venture, an experiment. Stepping out on a limb.

THE FIRST BOOK BY KONWICKI that I read is *Moonrise, Moonset*. I like it. The wit, the complaining, the cracks at the competition, the rooster struts, the confessions of weakness, envy, laziness, the flights into the past, back to the war (what war? what other war is there?), back to the Hollywood of the 1930s, forward to the films of modern times (he also makes films), more envy, more cracks, the man does go on, making fun of himself, of others, but making no bones about who he is: he's a real writer, folks, the genuine article, why he hasn't won the Nobel Prize or at least a stupid Academy Award is a mystery. *Moonrise, Moonset* is a memoir, a journal, a dustbin of failed fiction, a diatribe, a hoot, and a holler.

Then I read *A Minor Apocalypse*. It's advertised as a novel, and I suppose it is, but the narrator sounds just like Konwicki in *Moonrise, Moonset*. No problem about that. None. In fact I don't really care who is telling the story.

Narrator: You don't care about me? Look, I've got to set myself on fire. How would *you* like to be told you've been selected to douse yourself with gasoline and go up in flames?

He's sensitive, this narrator. Touchy. He's also *telling* the story. And if he ever does torch himself in the book, a miracle must save him. How else could he live to write about it? So all I mean about not caring, I tell him, is that I understand fairly soon I'm in a kind of parable or joke—a comedy—whose aim is to ridicule the Party, the System, the hacks, the crapola. So that's what I focus on: the message, the routines, the search for good Swedish matches, because when push comes to shove, you can depend on them. Ha, ha.

So that's all you focus on? K's narrator says.

No, I say. I have problems of my own. In the middle of reading your novel, where things become better for you as an artist (in my view), things become not so good for me in my personal life.

You are mixing fiction with fact, he says.

So what else is new? I say.

What happened to you? he wants to know.

My daughter fell in love with a Pole.

He sighs. So tell me about it. But be quick. Remember, I've been selected to go up in flames, a great honor.

I tell him I was living in Warsaw during 1987-88. That my daughter flew over to visit me, see a little of the country, and was romanced by a certain Jacek. When she returned to the States, they exchanged letters and tapes and—

Ah, tapes, he says. The living voice. Perhaps a measure of contemporary music thrown in. Loud, of course, with a heavy, head-throbbing beat. So it was serious. At least on the boy's part. I mean because of that head-throbbing beat, he says.

Then when I went home, I say, she wanted me to invite him over. Send an official letter to the US Embassy. She was in college at the time. I wanted her to graduate.

But you felt if you invited this Jacek over, she would be distracted from her studies. Better for her to finish school first, right? How soon would that be?

Half a year, I say.

An eternity, he says.

We nod and sigh.

So she pleaded, he says. She promised. And you, you gave in. And the boy shows up and naturally everything goes to hell. Right in the middle of your enjoyment of my novel. What rotten luck. I don't want to hear any more. Tell me, though, what were you doing in Warsaw?

Teaching at the University, I say, and coaching the city's baseball team.

Baseball! But this is insane. What was going on really? A CIA maneuver of some kind, right?

It *was* insane. We played on soccer fields, but the caretakers of the fields didn't want us to hurt the grass. They wanted us to spread canvas between the base paths, and on the pitcher's mound, in the batter's box.

At least, he says, give me a cigarette if I must hear this nonsense. Hurt the grass, bah!

I'm supposed to be writing about you. Your prose.

I hate my prose, he says. I hate it like a ghost, a bad memory, like pangs of conscience. Truly, what I produce is like some discharge oozing from my organism. As if it indicated that something were scarring over, that something were healing, but in fact nothing has scarred over, nothing was healed.

You are quoting yourself, I say. *The Polish Complex.* A crazy book.

Crazy? Merely a book about standing in line, he says.

Don't be coy, Mr. K., I say. You're standing in line in Warsaw in front of a state-owned jewelry store whose shelves are empty on Christmas Eve, for God's sake . . . huge banners are hanging everywhere proclaiming MOSCOW DAYS IN WARSAW . . . a terrorist in the crowd is trying to explain he's had a constant erection, night and day, since he was fifteen . . . a peasant woman with hard Nordic looks says she snagged an American billionaire, married him and, until he croaked, they jet-setted around Europe in their private plane (in the cargo hold of course they took along their two favorite cars); and now she is trying to get you, Mr. K., to come live with her on her farm—is willing to share you with your wife—while the terrorist, groping at her skirts, whining about his constant erection, is told by someone to go see a doctor for it; and someone else pipes up: he's seen plenty, none could help him . . . and you slip off for a drink, to harangue the reader, yourself, to confess your sins to a monk: Father, I lied, was jealous, I committed adultery, kept losing my faith and rediscovering it. But are those sins? Is God interested in them? Aren't they just our daily routine, the sad statistics of human existence? All this on Christmas Eve, Mr. K., in front of an empty state-owned jewelry store. Ha, ha.

Standing in line one meets people, he says. You lived in Warsaw. Didn't *you* stand in line and meet people?

In fact, I think I met your hard Nordic peasant woman, or her sister. I met her on a bus. She wanted me to run away with her to Rome.

Did you?

No.

Why not?

I explain all this is in some detail in *The Warsaw Sparks,* I say. But the short answer is: I opted to go play catch with George, one of my baseball players. He was having a problem with his girlfriend. It seems she was hosting a Russian boy she'd met in Leningrad. Poor George didn't know what to do except play catch with me, and later build another boat. He built model boats when he was upset. So far he had three: a fire ship, a tug, a cruiser. Now he figured he would build a hospital ship.

I thought, says Mr. K., that *I* was the focus of this piece you're writing.

Well, you asked me a question. One thing, as you know, leads to another. What do you think of George's ships? Their implications?

When a Pole thinks, says K., he gets sleepy. When he sees a balcony he wants to jump off.

The Polish Complex again, I say.

A book no one understands, he says. No one understands any of my books. They may understand faithfully translated major or minor sentences of mine; they may grasp the meaning of a metaphor, flickering moods; but they will not be able to empathize with my fate or embrace the meaninglessness in my meaning, which will seem to them unrealistic, alien, lacking motivation, and thus completely incomprehensible. They do not understand me because I am a Pole—

Excuse me, I say, but you remind me of my Polish son-in-law.

Your what?

That certain Jacek who exchanged tapes with my daughter, including tapes with head-throbbing measures, and then married her. She dropped all her courses at the university and declared for love.

Which you, as an American writer, are very much in favor of, he says. Love, I mean.

Of course.

But not of this marriage.

I asked only that she stay in school. I want her to graduate.

This is of course your practical side, he says. You Americans with your Puritan ingredient.

Why, I say, are so many Poles so fond of explaining America to Americans?

I am not fond of anything, he says. Maybe my typewriter, if I still have one. But after today the question is moot, because I will be nothing but a pile of charcoal.

An exaggeration, of course—Konwicki's remains would more likely resemble a lump of poorly cooked meat. Nonetheless we are silent for a moment, we hang our heads, as if practicing the act of paying our last respects to this imagined pile of charcoal.

It is difficult for me to concentrate. I glance around. I am being followed by the cops, the slick plainclothes types who all visit the same barber, same tailor, same rough proctologist for all I know. You can see them coming from a mile away. They even wear the same cologne—it smells like the stuff the really high-class Western hotels put in their toilets. The Poles call these cops stoolies, pigeons, Smurfs. I have puzzled these clones, confused them. Why would an American writer coach a Polish baseball team *for free*? Americans, they believe, do nothing for free.

Baseball! Mr. K. snaps out. Smurfs! Here I am, almost dead, and you can't even give me a few seconds of uninterrupted respect.

How did you know what I was thinking?

If I'm wrong, I apologize.

In any case, I say, I can't believe you'll be torched. For example, look at this last will and testament you prepare: "I bequeath my poor descendants who suffer from dandruff a proven remedy which will liberate them from their complexes and make them happy, even if only for a short while."

It must be followed exactly as I say, he says. Here is the prescription for the ointment:

> Ac. salicyl. 2.0
> Liq. carb. deterg.
> Sulfuri ppt. aa. 4.0
> Ol. Ricine 6.0
> Aoleps suille ad 40.0

And here is the prescription for the compound:

> Ac. salicl. 2.0
> Ac. biborici 2.0
> T-rae chinae 5.0
> Ol. Ricine 1.5
> Spir. vini 70 ad 100

Mr. K. looks at me kindly. Rub generous amounts of the unguent into your scalp, preferably before going to sleep, he says. It works. But watch out for your eyes. And wear an old towel or a plastic shower cap in order not to soil the pillow. In the morning, after washing your hair, use the compound.

Do you know how baseball works? I ask.

Still gazing at me kindly, he says, I would also like to bring up another hideous affliction. Constipation. It happens to even the most splendid, lovely, and spiritual of persons; sometimes it is brief, sporadic, sometimes horrible, lasting for months.

And such persistent constipation is able, shameful to say, to turn the most exalted existence into pure misery. I encourage those who trust me to drink a glass of cold boiled water upon waking. Dried prunes in the evening are also useful. At critical moments, when life is becoming truly disgusting, you should down a glass of booze in good company, but I point out that it should be no less than two hundred grams and preferably around three hundred.

In a baseball game, I say, you know exactly where you are—

Excuse me, he says, I must insert my genital organ into the genital organ of Nadezhda, this Russian girl whose grandmother was Lenin's lover. (I call him Grandpa, of course.) So please, give us some privacy when she arrives, at least turn your head. Ah yes, she arrives now . . . a girl with red hair supposedly inherited from her grandfather, a plump girl with fair skin, broad hips, one eye light green and the other blue-violet, a girl who sometimes goes walleyed and weighs around fifty-eight kilograms. Driven by our animal instincts we make love now by chance in a secluded ruin, on a staircase fouled by drunkards . . .

I turn quietly away. I stand outside and watch the red lights blink off and on atop the Palace of Culture, that Gothic gift from the Soviets. The Poles ridicule it. Young George, the smallest of the Sparks, dreams of hitting a baseball over that gray wedding cake of a building, a ball that will carry all the way to Moscow and land, boom boom, on Lenin's tomb.

By and by I feel a hand on my shoulder. It's Mr. K. looking sad, hangdog. Red-haired Nadezhda is nowhere to be seen.

Ah, Nadezhda, Nadezhda, he sighs . . . her red hair undone, her hand extended to me, her mouth open to cry out . . . . But nothing really happened. I held her. I inserted, she received. She hung on, her stiffened legs a millimeter above the burned floor, her inert feet brushing rhythmically against the brittle scraps of plaster strewn over the ground . . . a rapid chemical and electric reaction had taken place in her body, her own individual magnetic field had formed around her and synergized with my biocurrents. That was followed by a conventional spasm in the nervous system. But, as I say, nothing really happened, nothing.

Something came between you, I suggest.

Remember what happened pages before? When I glimpsed the gentle hills of her breasts? When I wanted very much to enter her and finally penetrated the warm and thrilling darkness? "Oh, God," she whispered. And at that moment the telephone near our heads gave out its shrilling, pounding demands— remember?—sounding like a pneumatic hammer.

You got up and answered it, I say.

Of course I answered it. I, the writer, was creating discord, cacophony, a great frustration, for wasn't Nadezhda's reddish hair—so full of life, so greedy, and spread out invitingly against the coarse gray blanket on that hospital or prison bed I had just left—a tremendous image?

You said *hello*. Your voice was hoarse.

Wouldn't yours be hoarse if you had just pulled out of a rich warmth? Anyway, it was Helena on the phone, one of those friends who had nominated me to go up in flames. She was out shopping for a gas can and wondered what color I wanted— there was a choice—red, yellow, or blue. Do you remember what I asked her?

Yes, if the color of the can had "a meaning," I say.

In our country tragedy often walks hand in hand with buffoonery, he says. In this I see our strength.

I had very sensuous dreams in Poland, I say. Shocking, deep. I attributed them to the sexy posters I saw almost everywhere, to my pretty students, and of course to the nature of baseball, its lusty thrust.

I love, he says, that ambiguous consanguinity, that risky symbiosis, that genius of people enchanted in two directions. Give me another cigarette, if you don't mind. I enjoy a smoke after making love, even when the act was pointless.

I light up too, remembering with pleasure a certain Warsaw beauty.

So what happened, he says, after your daughter married this Jacek? I am only asking because you were good enough to give me tobacco, and in order to put off as long as possible my fiery end.

There was a period of estrangement between us, I say. Then a thaw, a warming. Then a grandchild was born, Joanna. Now my daughter is back in college, finishing up.

And everyone, he says, is happy. Ah, America. Where would you be without the happy ending?

We would be lost, I say, without direction, values, religion, the will to go on. Therefore, whenever we suspect an unhappy ending, we close our eyes. Observe us discussing our literature (which word, by the way, should not be confused—though of course it is—with business brochures, profiles of candidates for political office, public relations manifestos and the like—e.g., "Here is some literature about our new line of frozen carrots"). My novel *The Second Bridge*, for example, though praised by a host of distinguished publishers for the writing, was nonetheless rejected for—well, let me quote one: "Most book buyers are women, and they want a happy ending, and yours is too sad." Sad to say, Mr. K., even at the University of Warsaw when I gave my students contemporary American novels that managed to avoid, let us say, happy endings, they frowned. They especially did not like to read about Americans living miserably in California, where the rainbow lands. My students said I was ruining their dreams. Mr. K., I see your eyes are closed. Have I put you to sleep?

A throbbing, he replies, is having its fun in the fissures of my brain. At the end of *Moonrise, Moonset* I predict that Poland will be saved by a miracle. Poland lives on miracles. To exist, other countries need good borders, sensible alliances, disciplined societies, but a decent miracle will do us just fine, I wrote.

Well, I say, you've had one, no? The recent free elections. The new government. The move to a market economy. You have goods on the shelves now, Mr. K. Luxury. Bright cars. Blenders. Billboards. No more censorship. Anyone can buy a banana, so to speak, an entire bunch!

We also have a demand for dreck. New lines have formed—not for poetry but for pornography. Those sexy posters you saw in 1987-88 were innocent adolescent fantasies, mainly nice healthy breasts, mere barbershop art for old duffers, compared to the shit that's available now.

Yes, but look at the big picture, Mr. K. To get something, you give something. There's no free lunch, baby. Besides, the quality stuff will rise above the muck. Our most seasoned commentators say so.

Do *you* believe that? he says.

Unless we poison the land and contaminate all the cows—a real possibility—the cream will always rise to the top, I say. I come from farmers, people who milked their beloved Belles and Bossies. I've seen how it works. Incidentally, I am also half Polish, so I know something about what Miłosz calls "an astonishing vital people who sink easily into moronic apathy and who show their virtues only in circumstances which would crush and destroy any other human group."

I am scheduled, he says, to burn in front of the Palace of Culture. At the end of the seventies this act had meaning. During the strikes of 1980 and after the imposition of martial law in December 1981, this act also had meaning. It had meaning—immediate meaning—for most of the eighties. Now what does it mean, my act? Am I dated? A relic? A crazy old crank simply trying to cross Marszałkowska Street with his blue gas can and Swedish matches and yelled at by wild-eyed drivers of new Western cars to get out of the way, get with it, get cool, watch where I am going?

But the Party, Mr. K., if you'll pardon the pun, is over. That cancer you describe in *The Polish Complex*—a cancer with a cosmic erection, a whorish lust for your ruthless neighbor to the north—is cured, canned, sacked, kaputski.

Listen, do you hear that? Children are singing Christmas carols!

There, you see.

Goddamn it, somehow it makes me feel sorry.

Sorry for what?

Doesn't matter what. Terribly sorry. I heard carols in the woods with the partisans. I heard them in prisons and I heard them with whores, but I never heard any that sounded like that.

Maybe even you are believing in miracles now?

What kind of miracles?

The kind that can never happen and never will.

To who? To whom?

To us here, us in general.

I've lost track of who's speaking.

I think you are, Mr. K.

In *The Polish Complex* . . . an old document . . .

Maybe in the present, the shops full, our eyes dazzled, the new products whizzing by . . .

Dick Hugo's Green Sportcoat

Glowing, that coat, and how proudly/defiantly he wore it the night we read our poems together—he and Madeline DeFrees and I—in no-kidding-glittery-watch-your-two-step-and-your-heartbeat-honey New York City. A long time ago: 15 May 1979.

Swimming laps this fall morning, a visitor in a Virginia college pool all mine, I had no trouble calling up standing on the sidewalk with Richard Howard, waiting for Dick's taxi to cut itself loose from a headlong Gotham column, slide over, and let that wary Montanan—and two-time National Book Award nominee—out. He emerged from the backseat back first—and what a back it was, covered with a garment whose bodaciously lime-green sheen surely had been mixed within the lower consortia of local habiliment-pushers and fomented forth to properly equip the out-of-towner for wherever he might wish to appear in style: Coney Island, Radio City Music Hall, Ellis Island ("Miss Liberty," he once wrote, "corroded with our green") or even—perhaps especially—on stage at the Manhattan Theatre Club to read his lean and burning poems.

Just before Dick turned from paying the driver, Howard whispered to me, "Nobody—nobody—could have invented that man." And when that man, this big guy from the Big Sky Country, greeted us with his roughneck-handsome, truly lovable smile,

I knew exactly what Howard meant, though putting that certainty into words would be tough now, if not ridiculously inadequate.

He meant, of course, the *poet*, the real McCoy, and that no one person could have done the inventing. Howard was simply underscoring a fact, one as true as a grizzly, the Bitterroot Mountains, or steelhead trout ascending rivers from the sea. A lot of people *helped* invent Dick Hugo—sort of, accidentally, fortuitously. Things happen and the poet notices them, or pieces of them, and he takes these atoms, so to speak, in: after a rubbing-while, some sparks fly around, or something like that, and *boom.*

Such inexact science is not exactly news, but this morning as I crawl-stroked up and down that beautiful pool the old news seemed, in its good old way, useful to me. We start out among the pieces—the broken, the fallen or about to fall, whether in cracked Northwest, cracked Italian, cracked *American*—feeling our way through the gray and toward the form that might receive us, redeem us, make us worthy in a new light, and then . . .

Madeline DeFrees and I had been invited to read with Dick at the Manhattan Theatre Club because of his recent book, *31 Letters and 13 Dreams*, published in 1977; one of the letter poems in that collection is to her, one to me, so the reading was titled something like "Richard Hugo and Friends." We were indeed his friends, and so was Richard Howard (there is a "Note to R.H. from Strongsville" in *31 Letters*), who I think introduced us at the Manhattan. My memory gets crowded here: blame the richness of the evening and its overflow; the collateral tranches de vie. O Life and its slices. R.H. might well have introduced us; doing so would have been typical of the generosity he aimed our way over the years.

And on that note of generosity . . . no, it's larger: on that *theme*, Dick's very seeable (no pun) sport coat, and his presence in it and in his poems as he growled/sang them, and how he bolted from his seat (*erupted* seems truer) to embrace Madeline and me immediately after we finished our turns on stage as if we needed protection—joined me all over again in a giant wrap, a complex stroke-and-kick, in good water for stretching out some, making my way, on a rainy morning just a whisper from yet another great mass of thrust, the Blue Ridge Mountains.

Well, why not? Montana, Rockies, Atlantic Ocean, Isle of Skye. Add the Cloisters, the Tavern on the Green, plus tiered, titled, romantic, and rank Yankee Stadium where my wife Judy and I that same trip went to see the Bronx Bombers' fireballing Cajun Ron Guidry out-pitch Detroit's Mark (The Bird) Fidrych before we sailed to Europe on the *Queen Elizabeth 2.* Then we drove up to Scotland and caught a ferry to Skye—where Dick had dug in for a recent spell among the apricot-colored Cuillin Hills and written about "the right madness" there, where we stayed in a Scottish castle owned and presided over by Colonel and Mrs. Macdonald. The ancient colonel even played "Amazing Grace" for us on his pipes. It was all almost too damn much—and yet what, exactly, *is* too much?

The good ship *QE2* was probably too much. I figured it might be. But Judy and I were trying to change the sad subject of a miscarriage for a while, and the consumption conspicuously at large seemed to be working. At our table in the dining room sat a charming man originally from Yugoslavia, an immigrant who had done well in the Big Apple and was traveling back to his birthplace, on vacation, with his Oldsmobile. He showed us photos from his wallet and told us, almost bubbling over, that "she" was in the hold, holding a full-fare ticket, because "I just love *Ah*merryka and I just love my car. She goes *ah*vrywhere I go, of course!"

In the title poem of Dick's *What Thou Lovest Well, Remains American* (1975), we meet Mrs. Jensen, "face pasted gray to the window," and the Grubskis, who "went insane. George played rotten trombone / Easter when they flew the flag." Such characters were no car-crazy Yugoslav immigrants, exactly, no seekers of delicious deluxe to be bundled in, escaping. Mrs. Jensen and the Grubskis, not to put too fine a point on it, went everywhere Dick Hugo went.

In Missoula, to this day, if you find yourself in the right bars at the right time with the right citizens, you just might hear how Dick, out fishing, would drive his big Buick as close to the water as possible, throw out his line, then settle into the comfort of the front seat, rod in hand, and wait. "Trout," the opening poem in *A Run of Jacks* (1961), Dick's first book, declares: "I envy dreams that see his curving / silver in the weeds." Declares: "I wedged hard water to validate his skin— / call it chrome, say red is on / his side like apples in a fog, gold / gills." Declares: "And I have stared at steelhead teeth / to know him, savage in his sea-run growth, / to drug his facts, catalog his fins / with wings and arms."

Anything wrong—contra naturam—so far? Quite the opposite: everything is gorgeously, dreamily right. I am not concerned with telling the truth here, certainly not the-whole-and-nothing-but kind (even were it possible) that might include a man fishing from the cozy womb of his car; but I am concerned with *constructing* a truth, an action that even opposing lawyers in any courtroom drama across the republic, minding their manners, will prove right beyond a reasonable doubt, over and over, when they stop the witness from blubbering on and on. A simple *yes* or *no* to corroborate *their* constructs will be just fine, thank you very much. But for the real McCoy in this truth business, the evidence left us by, among others, Mozart, Joseph Turner, and Emily Dickinson ("Tell all the Truth but tell it slant—") is far more satisfying for getting or getting *at* this curving, lovely, rotten, miraculous condition/place in which we find ourselves. With wings and arms you fly and embrace, if

you are in the Dick Hugo Construction Company; but know, too,
that you must pay and pay, and

>   play again
> and again Mrs. Jensen pale at her window, must hear
> the foul music over the good slide of traffic.
> You loved them well and they remain, still with nothing
> to do, no money and no will. Loved them, and the gray
> that was their disease you carry for extra food
> in case you're stranded in some odd empty town
> and need hungry lovers for friends, and need feel
> you are welcome in the secret club they have formed.

Dick could cock his head at an angle, an almost over-the-shoulder
aim, and say a poem he knew by heart as if firing it from a
cannon:

> You might come here Sunday on a whim.
> Say your life broke down. The last good kiss
> you had was years ago. You walk these streets
> laid out by the insane, past hotels
> that didn't last, bars that did, the tortured try
> of local drivers to accelerate their lives.
> Only churches are kept up.

More than once he fired this poem, "Degrees of Gray in
Philipsburg," accusingly at a New York audience, though not
the night he read with Madeline and me. I don't know why he
didn't. He still felt, despite dispensations from the Guggenheim
and Rockefeller foundations and all the other honors, an outsider
there. And likely always would. Maybe the lime-green sport
coat—the kind sold to a rube, a guy who looked like a truck
driver with his hair slicked back, an unsophisticate from the
hills—was another kind of shot, a commercial in full color. Is
this what you think of me? Well, have a good look. I can wear
it and wear it just fine. What's more, I like it.

Pick almost any Dick Hugo poem, and the degrees of gray around him—and us—are there. In the world. Does he really need to point this out? Unless our heads have been vacuumed and packed, don't we, especially now, *know*? He does more than just point, this lonely, insecure, empathetic roughneck from the rowdy West:

> Isn't this your life? That ancient kiss
> still burning out your eyes? Isn't this defeat
> so accurate, the church bell simply seems
> a pure announcement: ring and no one comes?
> Don't empty houses ring?

Listen. Where can you go when you're *that* lonesome? A dance? Another bar? To hang your head and feel the sweat sluicing down your ribs, your big feet stuck on the sidelines, heels hooked to a stool, afraid of stepping on toes, stumbling?

> This summer, most friends out of town
> and no wind playing flash and dazzle
> in the cottonwoods, music of the Clark Fork stale,
> I've gone back to the old ways of defeat,
> the softball field, familiar dust and thud

That's the "Missoula Softball Tournament," and only a game, sure; but if you really want in, heads up. Because here's where, taking your cuts at the plate, you can fail seven times out of ten and still make the Hall of Fame. Which hall of fame? How many are there? Sitting at your desk, in your car parked by the water's edge, under a whistling tree, or wherever you make your marks and rub your words putting things together—you know there are many, perhaps as many as there are good poems.

> Under lights, the moths
> are momentary stars, and wives, the beautiful wives
> in the stands now take the interest they once feigned,
> oh, long ago, their marriage just begun, years

of helping husbands feel important just begun,
the scrimping, the anger brought home evenings
from degrading jobs. This poem goes out to them.

Like a message wrapped to a pigeon's leg. Like a note rolled
up in a bottle. Spin that thing, round and round, for luck, for a
kiss to remember. Now, watch it slow down. The last out is
coming up, after which we can all go home, where we've been
heading—wanting to go—all along. Where we belong. For better,
for worse, or in between. Speaking a language as homely and
open and dear as all get-out. So, heads up, here it is:

Is steal-of-home the touching of the heart?
Last pitch. A soft fly. A can of corn
the players say. Routine, like mornings,
like the week. They shake hands on the mound.
Nice grab on that shot to left. Good game. Good game.
Dust rotates in their headlight beams.
The wives, the beautiful wives are with their men.

In the fall of 1983, almost exactly a year after Dick died, I
was in Missoula, recently back from living in Europe and on my
way to Portland to teach at Reed College. I was driving across
the country in a 1946 Chevy the color of eggplant. I wish I could
say that the radio, when it finally warmed up, featured Ella
Fitzgerald live at the Apollo, Benny Goodman and Lionel
Hampton going wild at Carnegie Hall, plus such wonderfully
lyrical ballpark crooners as Dizzy Dean ("He slud safe into
second!") and Red Barber—and all that sudden robust rich
cheering, those roaring rounds erupting like tsunamis to
acknowledge, praise, confirm. Dick's widow, Ripley, and I spent
some time walking around the hills, remembering, among much,
Dick's fondness for that old music, his mellowing, his arriving
at parties with his personal half-gallon of ice cream—often in
some god-awful sweet kid flavor like black cherry watermelon
bubble gum.

I asked about that sport coat, if he had worn it to the bars in town. Oh, yes. Oh, yes, Ripley said.

I'll bet he did, and I'll bet he looked like a million in it.

Six Fat Paragraphs

When I think of what Whitman means to me as a writer, I think of walking—stalking—around Izora Corpman's kitchen in Des Moines the summer of 1966. Six sheets of paper lay on the table, each one containing a summary of a short story I wanted to write. I had just arrived from Michigan, where for five years I worked on my first novel, annually rewriting it from start to finish, learning more and more about making sentences and scenes and getting closer to the story that lived so fine in my head but understanding, in the end, that those three-hundred-some pages would never become the true—or even a decent—translation of it. Now, in a new place, I put that novel away—away for keeps—grateful for the lessons it had taught me, that good long practice. I'd start another one, for writing novels was what I wanted to do. No, first I'd write something short, a few stories, build up my nerve. I had half a dozen ideas for short stories that I'd been carrying around. I would write those and *then* begin another novel. I was living that summer in Izora's apartment—she'd loaned it to me while she was away. At her kitchen table one morning, in a fever, I summarized my six story ideas in six fat paragraphs. Over the next few days and then weeks, I gazed at them, waiting for one to declare that it wanted to grow. None would. I was stuck with six fat paragraphs, slugs, clams, and I wanted to move, get going!

I went to a Catholic high school in Flint—a factory town—and all of my formal instruction had order, decorum, restraint at its core. In the spring of my last year at Holy Redeemer, the thing, the fact most on my mind, was my pitching arm. Which was no good any more. All those curves and drops and other twisting, tricky deliveries I had practiced since the sixth grade had produced, now, a stinging sensation whenever I threw. A future in professional baseball (scouts had charted my games for two years) was gone. In the midst of my gloom and self-pity, the English teacher gave us "When Lilacs Last in the Dooryard Bloom'd." The poem did not interest me. Death, death. "Come lovely and soothing death." "Laved in the flood of thy bliss O death." I wanted life. If anything in that poem struck close it was "O powerful western fallen star!" In which line I saw myself mainly, not Lincoln. But two years later, in college, I read for the first time "Song of Myself." It was spring. The season, the poem, those bold declarations! "Gentlemen . . . / Your facts are useful, and yet they are not my dwelling." There was also, nearby, a tall green-eyed beauty to whom I wanted to say many things for which I had no words. I borrowed Whitman's words, presented them to her. It was lovely, that chaos, that sweet education. But to write stuff like this was unthinkable—it had already been done—and yet the *courage* that Whitman flung around . . .

Now—1966—walking in Izora's apartment as if caged, I took Whitman from her shelf. "The spotted hawk swoops by and accuses me, he complains of my gab and my loitering. / I too am not a bit tamed, I too am untranslatable. / I sound my barbaric yawp over the roofs of the world." I looked at those six fat paragraphs again and thought—in a kind of heady desperation—maybe they wanted to be poems! Feeling cocky, a little crazy, released, I fussed over them and made what I thought were six poems, the first ones I ever wrote. I then went to the library and searched out magazines that published poems—poems that I liked. I sent my six poems, one each, to six magazines. (I didn't want to send all six to the same magazine because I didn't want to get them all back all at the same time.) One by one they were accepted and everything, or almost everything, became very different.

Stealing

The day I received the news of my father's death, I went to the store. It would be another day before I could fly to Michigan to be with my mother, sister, and brother, so rather than sit in a chair or pace or face the slow, dreamy May sky in my backyard, I got on my bike and rode to Safeway. To buy some groceries. To be useful, occupied.

My father died in his garden. A heart attack. He was sixty-four. I was thirty-five. He had come from farmers and lumbermen and was himself, by trade, a carpenter and, by love, a man who grew things in his backyard. He could build anything it's possible for one man to build—he had produced, from scratch, my mother's dream house—and with patience and water and an ongoing small-boy's wonder, plus German stubbornness when necessary, he could coax almost anything to flower. Even the green peppers he thought were bitter and would not eat but which my mother was crazy about. My own backyard, in Iowa, possessed a rich patch of wild black raspberries and some black walnut trees. Neither required much work from me, which was just fine. I was not a farmer. I was a poet.

I got on my bike and took a long roundabout way to Safeway, to buy some—some what? Some fruit maybe. I had nothing in particular in mind. *Going* to the store was the point, as if, I suppose, the day were ordinary, normal. And normally I went to the store on my bike; I didn't own a car.

I walked around the produce section, my favorite, and picked up a couple of things—an apple, an orange—and then I began going up and down the other aisles. It seemed I needed something else; I couldn't remember what. Oatmeal? Juice? Ice cream?

In the school supplies section, I looked at crayons, rulers, writing tablets, big bottles of paste, and then I saw a ballpoint pen, sky-blue. It was in a plastic and cardboard container, hanging with other pens on a hook. I removed the pen from the hook, broke it loose from the package and tried it out. I tried it out by writing on its cardboard backing the word I always write when I am testing a pen. "House, house, house," I wrote in a column.

I liked the pen and decided to buy it. I put it in my shirt pocket, then continued going up and down the aisles trying to remember that thing I seemed to need. If I saw it, I'd know.

But I didn't see it.

I returned to the produce section, filled a sack with peanuts in the shell (I remembered, filling the sack, how much my father enjoyed them), then I went up and stood in a checkout line. I saw among the magazines and newspapers there a headline announcing that a woman had given birth to a live goat and now wanted it baptized. Leaving the store, I wondered what name she gave it, what faith she subscribed to, who *she* was.

I was just about to get on my bike when a man approached me and asked if I would come back into the store. I said, "Sure." I wondered if he needed a hand with something. I followed him to a small room behind the meats section. He closed the door.

He said, "You didn't pay for that pen in your pocket."

I looked in my pocket. I'd forgotten all about the pen. He was right. I hadn't. I took out some money to pay him.

He said, "Not so fast, bud."

It was then, while he produced a paper for me to sign, admitting my theft, that I realized—understood—what was going on. But I wouldn't fully understand it until, five years later, I was in the middle of writing my novel *The Second Bridge,* and one of the principal characters, Bill Rau, completely to my surprise, begins shoplifting.

Bill Rau is going through an emotionally difficult and painful time. His perfect marriage is falling apart, and he is not, as they say, himself. As a novelist, I had to show that, dramatize it, not simply announce it to the reader. This is something the novelist knows by instinct, by *feel.*

Thus one day when I found myself writing, "Dried figs from Greece, fried grasshoppers from Japan, fillets of anchovies from Portugal, wild rice (extra fancy) from Ontario, kiwi fruit, sardines, crabmeat—these were among the things that slipped easily into his parka pocket and that on his morning walk to the supermarket he stole." I felt that Bill Rau was doing the right thing *because* it was wrong. He was behaving in a way he wouldn't normally behave.

The more I wrote, the better I understood just how significant his actions—and the items—were to the story: He is stealing food because, in a sense, he is starving; he is stealing food from faraway places because, subconsciously, he wishes to escape his unhappy circumstances, his present location, via Greece, Japan, Portugal, etc. It is also likely that he wishes—again subconsciously—to be caught in this unlawful act, to be punished for his failures as a citizen (*and* as a husband), and to be set straight.

Thinking about all this after I had written the theft scenes, I recalled the ballpoint pen incident in Safeway. Now an explanation for *my* act came to me—and as it came to me, I knew that Bill Rau's unlawful behavior was absolutely right.

I figured it was no accident that I had taken something from the school supplies section. I wanted, in a sense, to escape my adult present, be a kid again; and then, of course, my father would not be gone. It is also possible that I wanted, subconsciously, to be apprehended, wanted to be made to own up to something, face it, not simply get on my bike as if the day were normal.

The fact that I chose a writing instrument is also revealing, I think. In our work, my father and I both used such tools to make our respective measured marks, his on wood, mine on paper (a close relative). That the pen was the color of his sky-blue eyes told me even more, though what, exactly, is not, even now, easy to explain. Suffice to say I used that pen to write many lines, including these:

My Father after Work

Putting out the candles
I think of my father asleep
on the floor beside the heat,
his work shoes side by side
on the step, his cap
capping his coat on a nail,
his socks slipping down,
and the gray hair over his ear
marked black by his pencil.

Putting out the candles
I think of winter, that quick
dark time before dinner
when he came upstairs after
shaking the furnace alive,
his cheek patched with soot,
his overalls flecked with
sawdust and snow,
and called for his pillow,
saying to wake him
when everything was ready.

Putting out the candles
I think of going away
and leaving him there,
his tanned face turning
white around the mouth,
his left hand under his head
hiding a blue nail,
the other slightly curled
at his hip, as if
the hammer had just
fallen out of it
and vanished.

Tearing Down the Barn

Two weeks after my seventy-third birthday, I laid into my barn. It was Indian summer—early September—in Idaho's Clearwater Mountains. I smelled rosemary and plums. The Gospels yonder were so clear I fancied I might pick out elk browsing their peaks, hear bighorn rams butting heads. A crowbar and a hickory-handled hammer that I'd inherited from my carpenter father decades ago were my main tools. The leather pouch tied to my waist was for nails I pulled. Two stories, the barn stood among half a dozen massive pine trees—a pair of which had taken into their bark and meat the lip of the roof as they expanded. In a corner, where chickens and a pony once lived, a root had partially surfaced and lay along the dirt floor large as a python digesting a rooster.

Ten years before, I tore out the barn's first-floor apartment. A family of four had lived there while building their dream house a baseball toss away: a house full of windows and light, time-buffed hardwoods salvaged from condemned courthouses and schools covering the ceilings and walls, and a spiral staircase, all of which I happily bought when the family doubled in size and wanted to build a bigger dream house higher in the mountains. The apartment job I spread over most of the summer, removing enough each afternoon—after writing all morning—to fill my pickup and haul off, finishing the day fishing the South Fork for trout. The barn was a bigger job. I didn't think a lot about difficulties or dangers: I'd deal with problems as I came to them.

I knew where to start. I climbed to the roof—Montana at my right, Oregon at my left, Canada straight up the road—and plunged in. Maybe I'd get a poem or two out of the adventure. Or a story. If not, no matter. The real excitement I felt right then was over having, at this late date in my life, this big old barn, this gift, to tuck into. The rest—a new garage with guest quarters to replace the barn—was gravy, dessert.

The roof was a bitch. The former owner—Owen, I'll call him—had a reputation for being frugal, but he didn't hold back on the nails and screws he used to fasten down the large metal sheets: no big wind or big bad wolf was going to blow *his* roof off *these* pins. I had an old Craftsman electric drill that I'd bought at a garage sale in 1974, after seeing Mel Brooks's *Young Frankenstein,* because the drill came with a coffee can of bits the likes of which I thought I'd glimpsed hanging on the mad doctor's lab wall in Transylvania—none of which, however, worked for me now. (The can offered up other treasures: contributions I'd made to it over the years, if you cared to go digging for them, such as leaky bobbers, leaders tied in knots, and very sharp hooks so wound round with brightly colored yarns that salmon, I was told, would become enraged at such a gaudy display and could not resist taking a swipe at it—though none that I had ever met.)

I might have found a bit in town that would have zipped Owen's screws out, but finding such an attachment for my drill and then running an extension cord (probably a series of cords) up to the roof and minding it (no small matter working on a bias) did not seem worth the time and effort since I still had nails to remove. The crowbar did okay; a seven-foot length of two-by-four, with its larger fulcrum, did even better, but it was still slow going. I counted thirty screws and nails per sheet. These sheets were eleven feet long and almost four feet wide, and they overlapped. When at last I got one free, I gave it a push. I watched it slide off the rafters, acquire modest air, then glide to a landing area covered with pine sluff—like some great prehistoric cousin of the devilfish trying to live a life out of water.

Freeing three sheets was a good workout. I hunched over, kneeled, sat, kneeled, sat, and stood while digging at those nails and screws. Sometimes, perched near the roof's edge, I talked a little gloom to ward off falling ("Hic jacet a man a.k.a. Mr. Physics at the end"); sometimes, when a screw resisted mightily, I just muttered a string of vulgar nouns and verbs, and the more lyrical my string, the quicker the screw seemed to give up. When Michele came out with her camera, I might scramble to my feet, straddle the ridgepole, and, holding the crowbar like a microphone, croon à la Sinatra, "Come fly with me, come fly, come fly . . ."

"You, you—please be careful!" she'd sweetly call. I was, when you added up everything, pleased with myself, dopily happy, and feeling very lucky.

MY FATHER ONE MAY WAS walking behind a tiller, preparing his backyard Michigan garden for planting. My mother was in the kitchen making an apple pie, his favorite, and idly watching his progress through the window. She put the pie in the oven. When she checked on him again, he was lying in the freshly turned earth and her immediate thought was: *That silly man is taking a nap out there.*

She turned ninety-five a week before I began on the barn, a widow for forty years. She was still driving her own car, still living in the house my father built for her when I was in high school. I helped him on weekends and often after dinner during the week when he stretched and said he felt like hanging a few doors, knocking off a knotty pine wall—this after a full day at his regular job. "Won't take long," he'd say. As the nights grew colder, he'd finish his part faster and faster, then light a fire in the fireplace and fall asleep in front of it, his rolled-up coat for a pillow, while I finished my part.

A couple of years before I started tearing down the barn, my brother, Greg, who lives four or five doors down the street from her, got it into his head that Mom would be happier in an assisted-living arrangement. After all, he said to me on the phone, she's not getting any younger. I wished him luck. He researched all the possibilities in their area and found one, he called again to say, that he and Janet wouldn't mind moving to—they were both retired now and tired of mowing grass, washing windows, cleaning gutters, shoveling snow. The place he found had beautiful grounds—"tons of bonsai trees, lawn like a carpet and, get this, a twenty-four-hour water fountain that's lit up by colored lights at night."

When he sat down with my mother at her kitchen table to make his pitch, she stopped him before he finished his first sentence or even had the brochure open. Her eyes turned slitty for a second, and then she laughed, "Hey, Kiddo, what are you afraid of?" She had no time for little runt trees or any ridiculous fountain—had in fact a real busy day facing her, if he didn't mind. "If I didn't mind," my brother sighed over the miles between us. I could have saved him from his disappointment, I might have said, but he kept going, "Tell me what is wrong— what—*what*—with a water fountain lit up by colored lights?"

ONE DAY I REMOVED A sheet of roofing and discovered a bat lying still and smudge-flat on a rafter. Gone, I thought, either frightened to death by all the squawking the nails made when

I pulled them out (I wore earplugs) or had its breath pressed away by my walking on the roof directly over its head.

I like bats. I especially like seeing them cutting past, on the job, when I slip outside before bed to enjoy a fresh-air leak under a full moon. Looking at the little body, hoping it would suddenly come alive, I remembered a summer back in Iowa when I was awakened night after night by a fluttering above my bed. I'd get up, get my baseball glove, and turn on the ceiling light. As the intruder-bat circled the fixture, I'd catch it like a soft liner back to the mound and put it outside. Some nights I had to get up to catch two or three. After a few weeks all was quiet. Did I have one bat that got its kicks sneaking in nightly to land in my Rawlings, or did I have a family lost in the funhouse and I was their way out?

Anyway, it was one of the pluses of my life in Iowa, almost equal to getting around on a bicycle, not having to own a car. In moving to Idaho's panhandle almost twenty years ago, I'd had to buy a four-wheel-drive pickup, a compromise I hated to make. Now I was preparing to build a garage to house the pickup *and*, by and by, a car (electric, Michele and I figured), because the truck had well over 200,000 miles on it, and biking fourteen round-trip miles to town on a two-lane used by logging trucks was not safe, never mind practical, and... well... we were not getting any younger, as my brother—eight years my junior—was fond of saying. On the other hand, adding a carriage house over the garage with bath and kitchenette and finished inside with the barn's fir siding I'd pull off next—that made us feel better about all of it.

Plus, we got to stay home that fall, not go on tour for the first time in a coon's age. The previous fall Michele and I were on the road for two months and 8,416 miles, driving the pickup from Idaho to Utah, Colorado, Missouri, Arkansas, Tennessee,

Georgia, South and North Carolina, Ohio, Michigan, Wisconsin, Iowa, and back via St. Louis, Denver, and an icy Wyoming.

Glancing again at my bat (did it twitch?), I recalled we took four days off from the tour to relax on Georgia's Jekyll Island, walking barefoot along the Atlantic and swimming brisk laps in the hotel's unheated outdoor pool. We dined on fresh flounder, roasted pork belly with pureed beets, *boquerones*—oh yes, lots of tasty eats. (Tearing off a barn roof did work up thoughts of food.) But I didn't miss driving all those miles to read my poems and tell my stories over and over to college students, not when I could take out my earplugs and imagine hearing horny rams smacking each other for dibs on those juicy ewes chewing sideways on the Gospels, breathe in Italian plum scent, or do a quick double take seeing a bat I thought I'd killed suddenly lift off smooth as anything.

Then I uncovered a thick nest of stinkbugs. Their sudden-blooming, sinus-riling odor was dizzying, like a cheap sweet perfume whose formula the haywire perfumer had enriched with a defoliant. In the hands of a paranoid government it would make a perfect goad, I thought later, to use against the suspiciously unwashed who refused to come clean. A goodly number of these pale cricket-looking insects seemed dead and dried, but many were alive enough to sluggishly crawl over one another and spew away at me. I confess that for two seconds, had I been under arrest, I would have likely blabbed every secret I knew, if I could think of any. I made my way off the roof and stumbled pathetically to the house. At the door I called to Michele and asked if she had any nasal-spray products. She came to my rescue with a decongestant made by Western Family and soft murmurs to soothe the sufferer.

Avoiding the stinky roof for a while, I emptied the barn of my tools, mountain bike, rototiller, lawn mower, weeder, skis, all my fishing gear; of Mason jars full of screws, brackets, staples, and used nails not too crooked; of some gnarled driftwood suggesting snakes uncoiling, birds in flight, and other swirly motions that I'd brought up from the river over the years; of an ax-head I needed a handle for, a horseshoe, a rusty steak knife, and a kite one of my students at Reed College gave me nearly three decades ago and which I hadn't flown since; of the gray papery hornet's nest, big and round as a basketball but almost weightless, that my dog Henry and I found on one of our walks in the woods; of the dish Henry ate from that I remembered not knowing what to do with after he was killed; of the rickety whatnot I used for holding many of these things, the homemade FOR SALE sign Owen and/or his kids (probably his kids) had got up when they decided to sell their "Nice House and Barn on Nine Acres."

I thought of the "good haul" Huck Finn catalogs that he and Jim find in the two-story house floating down the Mississippi—including "a gourd, and a tin cup, and a ratty old bed quilt"—and I wondered, briefly, if I'd find me an old fiddle bow or a wooden leg. I took my accumulation outside to the little bit of corral fence I'd left standing a while back, for reasons I never got around to articulating to myself; maybe I just grew tired of pulling up posts and pulling off boards. I arranged everything along the twenty feet of fence so that later, when I constructed a lean-to using some of that barn roofing, my stash would have protection against rain and snow.

I SAT DOWN FOR A REST. What I sat on was the metal trap—the size of a mailbox—that allowed me to capture a pack rat alive. I could then transport the animal in my pickup to a site at least one mile from my barn (as the crow flew) and release it. Less than a mile, local wisdom claimed, and this large rodent would sniff its way back and resume collecting red bobbers, chartreuse yarn, shiny washers, tinfoil, and other bright objects with which to enrich its private cranny. (Resume, too, troubling my gray, green-eyed barn cat Yah teh.) I could not kill the pack rats I caught because my daughter Margaret—at that time just starting school—said that I couldn't. In summary fashion she would recite to me in words all her own my speeches about freedom—for rivers, wolves, ideas. That included pack rats, didn't it? "Besides, Daddy, they are so cute!" They were not cute; they had long hairless rattails and smelled bad— though otherwise they did resemble big cute squirrels, yes. Anyway, during the period that Margaret lived with me I trapped a couple dozen pack rats and gave them all their freedom a good mile away. I could still see the great joy in her face when we released that first one, for it exited the trap in a leap of Olympic splendor, followed by two or three Hollywood- level bounds on its way into the forest. Margaret named it *Packy*. She named all of them, and all of them lit up her expres- sion. When she and her mother moved to Moscow two hours north, I continued to live-trap and release.

Once I caught a skunk. Getting that critter out of the trap cost me a nice Pendleton shirt and a real Detroit Tigers wool cap that I couldn't wash the stink from with tomato juice or anything else. I really hated losing that cap—it took to my skull like those baseball caps I wrought for my persona in my youth, at once a nifty cap and a metaphor for all things that fit. After the skunk contretemps I was tempted more than once to drown any varmints that walked into my trap for the peanut butter- laced cracker, then move upstream and go fishing. But I didn't drown anything, remembering as I did Margaret's bright cheers as the pack rats burst, freedom-loving, into nature.

In recent years these smelly rodents have left me alone. Perhaps after I tore out the apartment in the barn and deer started coming in to lie in the old straw the rats became ashamed of their slovenly ways. But that's only a romantic guess. Yah teh also was gone. She had appeared one day at the barn door, a bawling, scrawny, ragged little thing with gorgeous emerald eyes and her ribs showing, clearly very hungry but terrified to leave the safety of the barn. Margaret, then four, sat in the grass a cooing distance away with a saucer of milk and sung the cat out. The name we gave her means *hello* in Navajo. Margaret was the only one to win this walk-on's confidence, but even for her there were limits—especially after Margaret held the cat in a cardboard box on her lap for a ride to the vet. Yah teh remembered that trip (and presumably something of the shots and the spaying) and would never take another. For the rest of her relatively long life, she would not go near the pickup—or any vehicle—*or* the house. The barn was her castle (which was why the pack rats irritated her so). One day Margaret, who came often to the mountain after moving to Moscow, was petting Yah teh and discovered some wounds. Something had attacked her, something that had to be big and fast and wily. Perhaps a week later I heard Yah teh on the deck outside my bedroom: she was hissing something fearful. By the time I got out of bed and turned on the outdoor light, the deck was deserted but for a rank, wild odor. I never saw Yah teh again.

If you no longer had a good barn cat, you had another good reason for tearing down your barn.

BY OCTOBER THE ROOF WAS off, the weather still fine—still T-shirt/flannel-shirt weather—and my appetite as keen as when I played three sports in high school. Michele, a very good cook, was feeding me Hunter's Chicken, fresh fish, and pasta in marinara sauces thickened with anchovies, chard from the garden, and onions and carrots deglazed with garlic and wine. Her rockfish garnished with a ginger-miso-sherry sauce and her sole under a white wine caper sauce were especially tasty on days when I missed throwing my line in the South Fork.

Our cherry tree and raspberry patch brought forth the fillings for cobblers, and the plum tree, sagging with issue, gave us all the plums we wanted to snack on plus a compote we poured over a buttermilk spice cake at night and over our breakfast oatmeal. On pancakes it would have been superb, but considering that I have favored oats to break my fast since puberty, Michele and I agreed it might be bad luck to change now while the barn-breaking was still in progress. Besides, oatmeal is easier to fortify with almonds and cashews and raisins and banana and fresh apple. I ate seconds at the evening meal (following a shower and the best bottle of ale anywhere) and slept in my bed (following a short spell with *To the Lighthouse*) for at least eight deeply satisfying hours. As a six-two high school senior I weighed 160 pounds; my football teammates called me Snake Hips. Fifty-five years and one barn later I would weigh 153 and stand, though the barn likely had nothing to do with my height, one inch shorter.

More statistics. The barn was thirty feet wide (counting one-story wings on either side), sixty feet long, and anchored to the clayey Idaho earth every ten feet by lodgepole pines. The second floor lay on forty pairs of twelve-foot planks bolted together to make joists that no four hundred pound local bears, finding themselves up there with an urge to rollick and roll, need fret about denting. The barn's siding, slated to line the future guest quarters, I would remove with care. The pines, cut into lengths for my stove, would warm us come winter.

The siding was easy to remove, but the boards took time to tidy. I'd drop a dozen or so into the yard, then kneel in the pine needles and pull any nails still in them, saw off moldy ends, and scrub away insect and spider leavings. The best scrubbers, I discovered, were the fist-size pinecones lying all around.

More than once, with all these boards around me, I thought about living in Gramps Gildner's lumberyard in northern

Michigan. My parents and I had been living on the top floor of a three-story apartment house in town, but one morning in my first winter an old man on the first floor fell asleep with a cigarette. My dad had already gone to work when my mother smelled smoke out in the hall. She grabbed her fur coat, wrapped me in it against the cold outside, and we escaped down the smoke-filled stairway. She kept going until she reached the new-car dealership in town (West Branch, a county seat, boasted just under two thousand citizens that year), where my dad ran the service department. At the precise moment she burst into his shop holding their six-month-old son swaddled in muskrat pelt, Dad was holding up the rear end of a Pontiac coupe because the car had slipped off the jack and he was trying to give his mechanic, who had been working underneath, some breathing room in his efforts to crawl free. My mother was crying, "Ted, oh, Ted," and trying to explain about the fire and escaping down the smoky stairs, her eyes burning. "But he just stood there, all blue in the face, that sweet man, and didn't understand a word I was saying."

Over the years, the exact make or model of the car my father was holding up by the back bumper got changed, and sometimes it was the front bumper; but the fire, the muskrat coat, pulling me from my crib, the smoky stairway, and running through the icy streets of West Branch to tell her story—these things never changed. I have alluded to this event elsewhere—in a collection of poems, in a memoir about my blacksmith-turned-farmer Polish grandfather who read Joseph Conrad translated into Polish, the only language my grandfather used—and I have told the story to live audiences more times than I could ever remember, trying not to improve it too much. But no matter how often the story gets told, by either one of us, at that moment it is always the truest account of how all my parents' wedding gifts (a large part of the story for my mother) and just about everything else they owned went up in flames, and how we came to live in a pine-scented apartment on the second floor of a lumberyard in the town where both my father and I were born.

Though my father was a good carpenter, he did not want to work for Gramps; a motorcycle-riding wizard with engines, he wanted, ultimately, to fly fighter planes. He and my mother had been planning to move to Detroit, where my father had hunting and fishing buddies who could get him hired on at the General Motors testing grounds. Then I came into the story, and they decided that the air quality and slower pace of West Branch made it a better place to be for a while. *A while* got longer, as it will, but, busy learning to talk and run, I was very happy living in Gramps's lumberyard during those last days of the Great Depression and the arrival of a time that seemed, in the whispers around me, both sad and very romantic.

A bit older, I harvested scraps of wood from underneath the big blue buzz saw for my Rube Goldberg constructions. I leaned close to hear the stories Gramps's men told of big bears, big trout, big Indian arrowheads—and which stream or cave they came from—and about sitting so still in the woods when the biggest buck they'd ever seen kept coming closer and closer, until the men thought they'd likely died and went to heaven and didn't even know it, which is why they never got a shot off.

You can damn well believe it or not, they'd say, licking their Bull Durham papers, rolling their own.

FDR AND CHURCHILL AND HITLER, saving bacon fat in a can beside the stove, nylon stockings impossible to get, songs about "over there" and not sitting "under the apple tree with anyone else but me," my Polish uncles in uniform, my dad rejected—three times—because of his heart murmur and his age, the balsa makings for model airplanes I pulled from my box of Pep cereal and which my dad helped me put together; my parents taking in a German refugee, Christina, who had been chased by dogs and slept in the Black Forest and managed, more than once, to escape just in time.

When the war over there was over, my mother and Christina cried and danced round the lumberyard with Gramps and Shorty and Ralph and Vi the bookkeeper and cooked lots of food, and then my sister Gloria (who was born right after Jimmy Doolittle's famous raid on Tokyo) and I went with our parents to a more official celebration, the big parade on Saginaw Street in downtown Flint, and we sat, one each, on our dad's shoulders. We had moved to Flint because our dad, who no longer wanted to fly Spitfires and Mustangs, took a job building houses for those who came home to sit with the girls and wives who had waited for them solo under that old apple tree.

All of this I called up from the clear-aired, smoky past while kneeling in the pine needles, pulling out nails, cleaning off my boards.

ONE DAY I FOUND A bottle that had contained, according to the label, a patent medicinal promising to alleviate seven kinds of pain, including heartache. Now it held six aggies and one purey. Another day I found a school report card for Owen's son from third grade that someone had stuck between a lodgepole pine and a fir board. The son's grades were very good, almost all *A*s. Was he holding on to something so precious he needed to hide it? The richest treasure from his last year in public school? A reminder of a time with the larger world and maybe a pretty teacher whose eyes and voice were soft and kind—a life before his parents turned to a certain philosophy, a certain highly restrictive way of making their way, and he and his five sisters learned their three *R*s at home? Those seven marbles in the old medicine bottle—what pains might they have helped ease as the owner knelt to draw his circle in the dirt? I thought crudely of the stranded cartoon character who throws his corked empty in the ocean, trusting the tides to carry his message home; of myself and all the notes I've thrown in the back of a drawer, waiting for a song to emerge. I wondered how long before the urge to be found—or to find our way under the bursting stars we never want to lose—goes away?

My dad died in his garden when he was sixty-four. My sister, Gloria, died at sixty-three while having breakfast with her husband, Fran. Her last words were, "Something funny is going on . . ." Like our dad's heart, Gloria's overwhelmed her. Years earlier the nuns who had long instructed her said much the same when, having departed from their care as class valedictorian and dutifully gone on, scholarshipped, to college, Gloria after two years quit the academy and announced that what she really wanted to be was a wife and mother. She married Fran, and in due time they brought forth four daughters and a son. (Almost the same issue in number and gender, I couldn't help but note, who once ran round and round the barn I was tearing down.)

FOR YEARS MY MOTHER WAS a faithful and colorful letter writer, but in her nineties she became more and more impatient with what she called her "loopy hand." So we turned mainly to the phone to exchange news, saving our penmanship for birthday and holiday greetings. I miss her excited run-on Faulknerian sentences very much, not least for those enriched lines and tropes that inspired some of my better poems. But over the phone she could still charm. On one call during the barn-breaking, she mused that the day might come when she'd be taking her Lumina out of the garage only to drive to the grocer's—"to have fun with that handsome young butcher they have behind the counter now, over the *fortune* he wants for his butterfly pork chops. A juicy one I might enjoy for breakfast, set my teeth into, I tell him, if it's not outrageously dear, dear.

I can make him blush and stutter every time," she laughed. "It's so cute. 'Oh go ahead, wrap up any old one your hand lands on,' I wave, 'I just sold a pint of blood to pay for it!'" This was right after the Detroit Tigers eliminated the New York Yankees in the 2011 American League playoffs. A Tigers fan since girlhood, she wanted a treat—which may have been the flirting as much as the chop—to celebrate.

"By the way, how's your barn coming along?"

"Just fine," I said.

"Don't get a hernia. Your brother had to have *two* sewed up on the same day. Boy, was he crabby."

But my mother cannot mention Gloria or her departed Ted so lightly. She will pause and go somewhere no one else can follow—she issues no invitations. Soon she returns . . . but never, it seems, completely.

HALLOWEEN WAS COMING, WHICH MEANT that Thanksgiving, my favorite holiday, was on deck. I love Thanksgiving because of all the kitchens I have been lucky to be in that smelled so homey and corny in the best way possible, and so sweet. The mountain was still warm and sunny. I unscrewed the nine bolts holding up the barn's sliding front door (big enough for a genius and his gig of mistakes to enter, or for a brace of ponies pulling their cart full of hay) and watched it hesitate a moment, then fall away—*soo-WUMP*—into piney duff. Ho! I dismantled this ponderous portal down to its parts. Then I stood on the plywood sheets nailed to the upstairs floor joists and removed the rafters overhead. Leaning extra body into my crowbar, I could feel the barn give back a little sway. Then I figured out where that genius-and-his-mistakes riff came from: Mr. James Joyce himself, who said, in *Ulysses,* "A man of genius makes no mistakes. His errors are volitional and are the portals of discovery." Then I went after the plywood.

The rafters and especially the plywood flooring took a while. During the first week of November, the weather suddenly turned cold and snowy—two or three inches of the wet, heavy stuff—and I had to shovel slush off every sheet I knelt to work on. My gloves and knees got soaked. At least I hadn't stuck myself on a nail yet, I thought—and within minutes of that minor crowing I drew blood. Twice. First in my left hand, then my right. Of course there's a law about crowing, which I violated, and of course the Band-Aids got wet and wouldn't stick.

I turned my attention to the electric power line that hung between the house and barn. Owen had supplied power to the barn by hooking into the house's line—his frugal way of saving on the cost of a separate line. He apparently never minded that 120-foot wire stretching overhead between the two buildings. It was, near as I could tell, the only above-ground electric wire for miles around, vulnerable to high winds and falling trees and tree limbs. I had wanted to get rid of it for years. Fishing, swimming, a garden to tend, fruit trees to plant, a hike in the timber, going after stories and poems—always something to distract me, until now.

I'd turned off the power at the breaker in the barn and cleaned out all the wiring inside, but from the house to the breaker the line was still hot. I thought briefly of cutting all power to the house, thus rendering the line to the barn safe to take down. Then, biting the wrappers off yet another pair of Band-Aids, I thought that I'd be smart to call an electrician.

I consulted the Grangeville phone book. The town, seven miles from my house, is the seat of Idaho County, which stretches from Oregon to Montana across the Idaho panhandle, is geographically as big as New Jersey, and has one stop light against a lot of fish, trees, game animals, and cattle. That stoplight is in Grangeville, where Jim Spruell, journeyman electrician, lives. At the moment he was working in Lewiston, an hour north, rewiring an elementary school. But he'd be home for the weekend—his first weekend off in months, he told me—and would call me on Sunday.

After lunch on Sunday, as promised, he called and said he'd be right over.

"On your first weekend off in months?" I said.

"You're not in immediate need?"

"I am."

"Okay then."

He pulled up in his pickup, with a big yellow wolf-looking dog riding in the open box. I was in the yard, waiting. Jim is six foot five, well over two hundred trim pounds. He was wearing Bermuda shorts, a T-shirt, and running shoes. I was wearing a wool watch cap and a jacket over my flannel shirt. I thanked him for coming right over.

"The job calls, I go. I go everywhere. Only bad part's motels. I hate 'em."

"Nice looking dog there," I said. "What's his name?"

"Dog."

"Dog?"

"Somehow it fits him."

"You play basketball in school?"

"Boxed and wrestled. B-ball was too slow."

He looked at the power line I wanted down, saw how it came out of the house and was stapled under the eaves on its way over to the barn. He checked out the breaker box in the barn, the main box in the house. Then he got on top of my woodshed, which is attached to the house, and began to pull at the power line stapled under my roof. He produced a pair of nippers. I *think* he slipped on a glove.

"Hey! Don't you want the juice turned off!"

"Where's the fun then?" he said, cutting the hot line into manageable lengths and throwing them down for me to gather up. In less than ten minutes he took out the entire line and cleared the way for me to resume removing my barn without frying myself. At his truck, he said to give a holler when I was ready to wire my garage and guesthouse.

AFTER JIM SPRUELL AND DOG left, I pried the last of the plywood off the second floor, then began on the stairway, made of planks, that led up there but was no longer of any use. Chuck Davey popped into my head—no doubt because Spruell had mentioned boxing. Davey had gone to Michigan State, as I had, and was for a time considered collegiate boxing's brightest star—and maybe still is in those ever-dimming corners where old men have such thoughts. He won four NCAA titles (unprecedented) and was a member of the 1948 Olympic team. In 1949 he turned pro: he was twenty-four, a lefty, a stylist, Irish-fair, and—not that it mattered much in the ring, but it was colorful to hear—in possession of two college degrees, a bachelor's and a master's. TV boxing fans in the early 1950s loved him. They knew, as my dad and I knew—as the movers and makers in the game knew before any of us—that a challenge from Davey for Kid Gavilán's welterweight crown was inevitable. And when in 1953 the fight came to pass, between the unbeaten southpaw craftsman and a man who had cut his hard way out of the sugarcane fields of Cuba by perfecting a deadly up-from-the-knees bolo punch, the event was called, naturally, a natural.

My dad and I watched it on our 21-inch Muntz. For two rounds Davey did a dance-and-jab and Kid Gavilán stalked him. In the third, Davey suddenly was down—for the first time in his career. He got up and reached the tenth, but along the way he suffered, especially in the fifth and sixth rounds. Gavilán switched to left-handed—"just for fun," he said later, but the mockery during those rounds was clear. Davey may have defeated Ike Williams, Rocky Graziano, and Carmen Basilio—two former champions and a future one—but now he was in the ring with his master. In the tenth, after a flurry of punches from Gavilán so fast not even the ringside commentators were sure what had happened, Davey stood bent over at center-ring holding his gloves to his face. The ref put his head close to Davey's as if to hear his confession and counted him out. Later we learned that the terrible bolo had landed on Davey's Adam's apple and he was struggling to breathe.

Davey had nine more fights and lost four, including three defeats in a row. Word was, Gavilán had all but finished him off; he should take his education and go use it. In October 1955 Davey fought somebody named Alan Kennedy in Lansing, Michigan, an easy jog from the autumn-scented campus of MSU where the leaves on the hardwoods were turning and falling, and where the Chuck Davey story had got such a marvelous start. He outpointed Kennedy, retired, and went into the insurance business in Detroit, his hometown. He was thirty years old. In six years as a pro he won forty-two fights (twenty-six by knockouts), lost five, and had two draws.

Just about two years later, I was a freshman at MSU in John Brotzmann's boxing class. Brotzmann also coached the Spartan team, and I was thinking I might try out for it *if* I didn't make the basketball team. I was only a tad cocky, thanks to my high-school successes in Flint and the young Holy Cross sisters—my teachers—who had had *their* particular confidence honed in South Bend under the Golden Dome of Notre Dame, a confidence that for many of us was contagious. I thought I could get down to 147 pounds. As a welterweight, with my height, I figured I'd have the reach to stay out of trouble and, weaving and dancing like Davey, a good chance to win on points.

One day Brotzmann announced a special guest, who got loose skipping rope and rattling the small speed bag. We watched in wonder. It was of course Chuck Davey. When he groaned,

"Coach, I'm in shitty shape," he might have been glossing Lear. When he said he hadn't put the gloves on lately—"only weight"— we thought, *Is he kidding?* Okay, we could see a tiny roll above his waistband. Also—despite a reputation for slipping a lot of punches—he carried noticeable cauliflower about the ears and slightly puffy cheekbones. Never mind—look at the *blur* he made of that small bag!

The retired fighter and Brotzmann climbed through the ring ropes and Chuck, an all-mick smile across his chops like the one James Cagney flashes tap dancing his noodle nearly off in "Yankee Doodle Dandy," put together a number of combinations against the coach's hands, in slow motion, to show us how it was done.

Jabbing my crowbar under yet another stairstep to lift it, I had to smile too. I knew what was coming. I would climb through the ropes, a puffed-up freshman, and pursue, because Coach Brotzmann told me to, a recent challenger for the welterweight championship of the world. He said, "Let's see you get inside that left hand." I pounded my big pillowy gloves together, leaned into my toes, and tried to make contact with Chuck Davey. I could not touch him with either hand—he was that quick at not being where I aimed. I almost lowered my head like a mad little bull calf and crashed into him.

I knew two things quickly: I was honored to be there, and I was a clumsy, hot-faced fool. Pausing with my crowbar all those years later, I remembered how my chest hurt from breathing so hard, how I nearly cried when Brotzmann called, "Time!"

AFTER THE STAIRS WERE GONE, I looked up at a corduroy-like lay of joists a couple of feet overhead, running the length of the barn and supported around the periphery by lodgepole pines looking like stilts. I avoided walking underneath this skeleton—a really good wind, such as we sometimes got at four thousand feet, might knock it all over. We had an eighty-one-mile-an-hour wind a few years back that caught the edges of four sheets of metal roofing on the house and curled them up like the tops on tins of anchovies. The more slender seventy-five-foot pine trees near the house bent and swayed and whirled around like dervishes.

I wanted those floor joists down on the ground. All of them. I couldn't see trying to drop only one at a time: the skeleton—still a great mass of weight—was too dicey to work underneath, or even at the edge of, with my crowbar. Pressing one joist to let go, I might encourage several to come crashing down on me.

What to do? I was mulling this problem when thoughts of Chuck Davey returned.

We were sitting, he and I, at the bar of an Irish eatery near Tiger Stadium, the beautiful old ballyard that would be abandoned many years later. It was 1962. As a member of the Detroit Sports Broadcasters Association, I was attending the group's weekly lunch, an event that featured a guest athlete—typically a Tiger, a Lion, a Red Wing, or a Piston, who had done something grand recently and could be persuaded to break bread with us and, well, be sociable. Because, basically, it was a social hour or two, in which we chummed with a star and picked up some color.

Chuck Davey had dropped in for a beer and a sandwich. Eight-by-ten glossies of him and other battlers who had found fame in the Motor City—Joe Louis, Ty Cobb, Mickey Cochrane—hung on the wall beside us. The former challenger had not entirely retired from sport. He had a hand in promoting an amateur boxing event sponsored by the Detroit Athletic Club, the Chuck Davey Classic, which raised money for nonprofessional programs around the country, and he was taking up, he told me, a little running to lose some pork.

He looked more marked than five years before when he turned that speed bag into a buttery blur. The cauliflower ears and the facial puffiness told more soberly now, as we sat side by side, what kind of punishment he'd been trading in not all that long ago. And Kid Gavilán's bolo punch was clearly present in his raspy near-whisper, though you could hear him fine if you leaned closer. Sure, he remembered that MSU visit. I asked if he remembered the student clumping after him almost flat-footed, unable to catch him?

"*You?*" Davey laughed. He clinked his glass against mine. "Listen, kid, how'd you like to come work for me, get your feet wet in the insurance business?"

A ROPE, I THOUGHT. I COULD lasso one of those lodgepole pines at either end of the barn, tie the rope to my pickup, and pull to see what happens. I'd pushed on a corner lodgepole—pushed hard—and felt the skeleton move more than a mite. Maybe I could pull at least part of it down. But I didn't have a rope. I had a garden hose. I looped it around a corner lodgepole, high up, held the two ends together and began stepping back from the barn—to see if I had enough hose to let me reach a safe distance. To test the hose, I gave a trial pull. The lodgepole came toward me. It was falling. Everything was falling. Those lodgepole stilts spaced every ten feet and holding everything in place gave way domino-like to send at me en masse all the skeletal parts of a big barn stripped of its skin and as fast moving, my eyes said, as a tidal wave or a grizzly bear or—this actually visited me once—the giant jowly face of Don Rickles I stood frozen in the path of in a really sweaty nightmare.

From that test pull on my garden hose to the end took maybe five seconds. All those joists lay side by side in the dirt, in a row military-neat, almost as neat as when they were ten feet up. Michele came running from the house.

"I *heard* something!" She hugged me. "But you're all right!"

I was very all right. The lodgepole I'd looped fell close to me but only close enough to help me see sharper, feel lighter, for a few moments.

"The house jumped!" Michele said.

"Jumped?"

"Or maybe I jumped," she laughed.

OVER THE NEXT COUPLE OF days Michele helped me separate three pairs of twelve-foot planks bolted together. She held a wrench on a bolt's head, to keep it from turning, while I turned the nut. The stubborn, near-frozen bolts—five per joist—were infested with a bright brown powdery rust that possessed a mighty greedy bite, so the going was hard and slow. At first we laughed at our groaning; then the challenge was no fun at all. I could see us spending weeks on those bolts.

I needed to break the joists into manageable pieces; intact, they were way too long and heavy to carry to a burn pile—if I had wanted to burn them—or to load in my pickup and haul away. Before I had them on the ground, I thought maybe I'd use my chainsaw to cut them up; but once I could inspect them closely, I saw they were practically festooned with nails, even with some spikes, and finding a safe route to run my STIHL was not easy. The planks in each pairing were kept about an inch apart by small blocks of wood helping to hold each bolt, and checking for nails in those narrow between-planks spaces was a problem. Imagine a cartoonishly long sandwich made with two pieces of bread held together at intervals by five toothpicks, each toothpick stabbing a small rectangle of grilled tuna, the sandwich's only filling. These five samplings of tuna of course keep the two slices of bread from touching each other. (An absurd comparison to a dusty floor joist, but I was hungry when I assessed the problem.)

On my knees I carefully searched a joist for nails, managing to find places between the bolts where I thought I could probably saw safely. Holding my breath with each cut, I broke that joist into four lengths I could carry to my trash pile. I then went after the others.

TAKING ON HIS SENIOR YEARS, Chuck Davey was running marathons and swimming. One day he dove in the ocean—just down the road from me, it seemed. I was hiking up the mountain, raising a sweat, he was slapping at big waves rolling in—each of us trying to stay in shape, as the phrase has it, the phrase that came to me when I heard what had happened. He'd been slammed ashore by a wave and suffered a snapped vertebra. A bigger blow than Gavilán's, it left him paralyzed from the neck down. He was seventy-three.

Though he'd been known in the ring as a craftsman who chalked up points to win, the record shows he knocked out the majority of his opponents. That fact came back to me then, as a reminder of his strength.

Davey hung on for four years, then left behind his wife, Patricia, and their nine children. If I had had a boxing career like his, I've caught myself musing, I might have wanted a bunch of kids too. For the bustle and warmth, mainly, but also to help balance things out, you might say, between the ring world and the real one.

I LOOKED AT MY PILE OF barn parts waiting to burn, a kind of sculpture, a cluster of struggling souls fallen together, reaching. That job offer. Not a big moment—I wasn't interested in trading my writing life for insurance. But when I thought of him, more than once, enjoying the story of Chuck Davey not being where I aimed, I felt charmed, happy all over settling down again in an old leather chair worn just about perfect at the long plywood desk I built almost fifty years ago—and where, right after breakfast, as usual, I gathered my supply of sharpened pencils and went to work.

A Very Small Cemetery

Border Days in Grangeville have been held annually since 1911. Three days—July 2, 3, 4—of parades, cowboy breakfasts, pretty girls on horseback, and the oldest professional rodeo in Idaho. Pioneer Park at one end of town is given over to bluegrass pickers, jewelry makers, landscape painters, another church stepping up (a different one every year, it seems) to push the *best* strawberry shortcake *anywhere*. Heritage Square downtown offers opportunities to show off your softball throw, put your tots on kiddie rides, watch crazy teens go wall climbing, or to brave eats not normally tried in these parts, plus your usual burgers and dogs. Over at the rodeo grounds a country baritone behind the mike brings out the next bulldogging, bronc-riding, calf-roping event: "Let's getter done!" Now and then a participant is whisked away by an ambulance, applause for him chasing after the siren; but only once has anybody been killed—a cowboy from White Bird down the road was thrown and kicked in the chest by a bronc a few years back.

Where the Border Days notion came from depends on who's talking. It might could be, as some put it, a celebration of settling a border dispute with Oregon or Montana, or with the Nez Perce, or some combination of these neighbors. Possibly Border Days celebrates Idaho entering the Union on 3 July 1890 and folks up here in the panhandle needed a couple of decades to get excited about the idea. Some long-time locals still can't get excited and during the hoopla go off in the woods with their tents.

In any case, a good many people born here who moved away come back for Border Days; they stroll Main Street and check out all the old photographs put up over nearly every inch of storefront glass and squeal at seeing themselves so skinny, finding a teacher they liked, picking out that dopey first boyfriend, the girl who married the rancher and had six damn-fine-looking kids. School reunions are organized around Border Days. The Chamber of Commerce reckons this single week clears the goods off many a shelf and fixes tons of potholes. On the last night, after the dust at the rodeo grounds has settled, folks and kids not worn out yet spread their blankets on the grassy slope below the school track and *oooh* and *aaah* at the fireworks show. The whole thing (except for a rare black cloud like the death of the White Bird cowboy) makes people feel part of something fine—exactly what, it's hard for them to say. "But what the hey, look at who finally turned up!"

AFTER A HOT DAY WORKING in the garden or slapping fresh cedar stain on the house, I clean up, then open a bottle of India Pale Ale. I said to Michele once, "I prize this ale. I will miss it when I am dead."

"Nora Ephron says she will miss pie," Michele said.

"The one about a circle and its distance?"

"I believe the one you eat with a fork."

"I will miss all kinds of measurements, mysteries, and tastes," I said.

HERE IS A LOCAL MYSTERY—ABOUT a likeable, attractive woman with a great smile named Laurie Rockwell. Laurie served as executive director of the Syringa Hospital Foundation in

Grangeville. Over a three-year period—2008 to 2011, when the stock, housing, and many other markets were hurting bad—she embezzled almost $200,000, according to the Idaho Attorney General. In a town of 3,141 (2010 census), no one, apparently, suspected anything funny—neither her fourteen-member board of directors nor her husband, James Rockwell, owner and COO of a local E.K. Riley franchise.

James and Laurie and four of their five children live in a large house they built shortly before the pilfering. Around the same time, James purchased a former clothing store on Main Street, basically tore it down, and put up a modern stone-and-glass structure with space for his financial offices, plus space to rent out. If he could find good renters, he said one day, showing me around.

Previously, James worked in a small office in Grangeville's first E.K. Riley franchise, two blocks down the street. In town to buy groceries at Cash & Carry, I sometimes walked across Main Street and sat in his comfortable visitor's chair. He and I were on the board of Sts. Peter and Paul Catholic School. He was a member of the parish. I wasn't, but my daughter Margaret attended Sts. Peter and Paul; after school she played with the Rockwell kids. When James had learned that I graduated from a Catholic school in Michigan in the 1950s, at a time when parochial schools were staffed almost exclusively by nuns and the students typically wore uniforms, he asked if I would consider joining the school board. He and Laurie and other parents were keen to dress the students in uniforms—an idea that was meeting with resistance, some of it fierce. The pro side liked uniforms because they were an inexpensive, practical way to clothe the kids and, in the bargain, eliminate that sometimes neon-bright divide between kids who wore nice new clothes and kids whose parents could not afford nice new clothes.

In favor of egalitarian measures, I joined the board. Many assumed I was a practicing Catholic. The pastor knew otherwise but said nothing, perhaps hoping I would come clean and make my Easter Duty. He favored uniforms, but mindful of conservative parishioners mumbling about threats to individual freedom and creeping socialism, he broadcast peace from the pulpit. Quietly he urged the pro-uniform group to stick to its guns.

Laurie's committee proposed uniforms of khaki, blue, and white: trousers and polo shirts for the boys, skirts and blouses for the girls. Still, parishioners mumbled. One fought the board on this issue as if his life were at stake, sending his wife, who favored uniforms, in tears to the pastor. The pastor invited her and her children to move into the convent behind the school, empty since the last nun had died. The tearful woman accepted.

The board voted to adopt uniforms but, to avoid serious trouble, held a parish-wide vote; the pro-uniform side squeaked to victory. Laurie drove to Lewiston with a list of sizes and color preferences and negotiated a discount with JCPenney. Parents who were strapped paid nothing for uniforms, the parish picking up the bill.

I LIKED STS. PETER AND PAUL School. The building contained only four classrooms so the sixty-some students in the eight grades were grouped thus: grades 1 and 2, 3 and 4, 5 and 6, and 7 and 8 were combined. The older kids in each pairing got to act as mentors, passing on to their younger classmates what they had learned the year before, creating an intellectual camaraderie. I liked the student-teacher ratio—about fifteen to one. I liked the teachers, all lay, who invited me to visit their classes anytime and who struck me as educators first, dogma-pushers a respectful second. There were no discipline problems. Margaret was happy at Sts. Peter and Paul for three years, then her mother decided they needed to move to Moscow. I retired from the board and saw the Rockwells less and less.

What gave my relationship with James and Laurie an extra tick was that we all had lived in countries deeply scored by Communism. James gave me to understand that we had a special bond, a honed insight into evil, due to my living in Poland before the Berlin Wall came down and in Czechoslovakia soon after, and his and Laurie's time in Vietnam after the war there. Early in their marriage, they operated a Hanoi glove factory, he told me.

"What kind of gloves?" I asked.

"Oh, ski gloves, work gloves," he said.

James had read *The Warsaw Sparks*; he liked how I describe the difficulties the Poles faced making their way under a system they hated. He, too, hated that system. But he did not make speeches against it; indeed his references to politics in my presence—in the beginning—were sparse and usually muted. (My politics in *The Warsaw Sparks* are clearly liberal.) By and by, he let me know his by explaining why he had dropped out of Seattle University: "To help Walter Hickel become governor of Alaska." Hickel, a Republican, was still a player, James said, adding that he had Hickel's phone number—had a lot of phone numbers—implying he could reach some pretty important people.

James also let me know that he and Laurie had written a book about their Vietnam experiences and asked my advice about getting it published. I told him how to query editors and agents and warned against vanity presses. He never asked me to read their manuscript, and I never offered. They sent it off to publishers a few times and then gave up. Rejection was not easy for James. Asked how things were going, his response was always, "Great! Just great!"

In town James wore a dark-blue blazer, rep tie, white shirt, and tan slacks, a high mahogany shine on his tasseled shoes.

His closely shaved jaws also shone, and his short dark hair always seemed fresh from a barber. Once, low on firewood, we went into the winter woods and cut down a dead red fir to share, and several times we took our kids mushroom hunting. He wore jeans on these occasions and looked awkward in them, off his confidence. At the house he and Laurie rented before they moved into the new one, he proudly showed me a wood cabinet he built for drying mushrooms. I admired it. He built the cabinet in a shop class before he left to study—briefly—with the Jesuits in Seattle. He coupled his story of dropping out to work for Hickel with stories of the rampant student drug use he claimed to have witnessed and clearly did not approve of. Here, he did make speeches. "They injected themselves with anything and anywhere. Even in the eyeballs!"

James's father, Dr. John Rockwell, a respected Grangeville physician, was long retired—and suffering from Parkinson's—when his daughter-in-law began stealing from the foundation. He and his wife, Blanche, lived with James and Laurie in a private wing of the big new house. Laurie's son Chase, from her first marriage, was living there until he graduated from high school. He was attending the University of Idaho in Moscow during his mother's unlawful withdrawals. James ran, as a conservative Republican, for one of the three seats on the Idaho County Commission and won, I think, without breaking a sweat.

In office, he backed a proposal to build a landfill in a pretty hayfield three or four baseball tosses from Pioneer Park that would have brought garbage trucks from four (possibly five) counties rumbling through Grangeville at an ugly clip of no fewer than five hundred tons of waste around the clock every day year-round for a projected fifty-year period; but even worse, the hay field covers a portion of the Columbia Plateau aquifer system supplying fresh water to 44,000 square miles of eastern Oregon and Washington and western Idaho.

James heard such loud objection—including threatening phone calls from his own livid base—he no doubt began to sweat. There was also a lot of hate mail, he told me, when I called to ask why he supported such a bad idea. His fellow commissioners, also Republicans, felt the heat too, and all three backed off a landfill in Grangeville. When news of the devastating assault on the foundation first broke in the conservative-leaning weekly *Idaho County Free Press*—on 30 March 2011, almost two months after the crime was reported to the sheriff—Laurie's name was not mentioned; it didn't need to be since her replacement *was* mentioned—at almost the end of the story. As more than one citizen said—in so many words—"If you listed everyone in town and *had* to rank them according to who *might* do something like this, starting with the most likely, Laurie Rockwell's name would be dead last." The news was incredible, way beyond what almost everybody called the colossally dumb landfill idea. *Why* would she do it?

Thirteen months later, on 11 April 2012, the *Free Press* reported that Laurie Ann Rockwell faced five counts of grand theft and five counts of computer crime "on allegations she embezzled thousands of dollars" from the Syringa Hospital Foundation. Due to a conflict of interest—her husband's public office—the Idaho Attorney General's Office would prosecute the matter.

In a box in the middle of this front-page story, in boldface type, James declared, "I turned her in." He goes on to say (aware of rumors in the community) that he also turned over to investigators all of the hospital's computers and files in his wife's possession, plus copies of his and Laurie's personal bank accounts. He says the investigators "didn't ask; I offered, and I delivered [these documents] to them. [. . .] That was fourteen months ago."

In the main story, he says he took Laurie to St. Joseph's hospital in Lewiston, where she was diagnosed with manic depression. "I try to comprehend this; I can't. It is simply impossible to comprehend mental illness." He says he prays for Laurie. "We are defined by how we deal with challenges. These dark days of challenge give me the opportunity to live my faith without judgment and to be there for my wife, to honor my vows to her, through good times and bad, sickness and health, till death do us part. I will be there."

Two weeks later—on 25 April 2012—a letter from James's mother, Blanche, appeared in the *Free Press*. "Doctor Rockwell and I love our son, James's wife, Laurie, as our own daughter, and we, of course, are here for her during this ordeal." What follows—the bulk of her syntactically awkward letter—is devoted to reminding us of her husband's career in Grangeville (41 years), how much Syringa Hospital meant to him, the lifelong friends he made there, and how overwhelmed the family has been "by the outpouring of good wishes, solidarity, love, and prayers."

In these public declarations were James and his mother, some citizens wondered, steadfast, loving relations, sensitive to life's twists and mental turns, or was a story being shaped about one crazy operator? "How many husbands do you know would *turn in their wives* and then go to the newspaper to have it *broadcast?*" was a response you heard in more than one quarter in the seat of Idaho County.

On 25 July 2012, almost four months after she was charged with those five counts of grand theft and five counts of computer crime, the *Free Press* ran a story well inside the paper and below the fold, saying that, in a plea deal, Laurie A. Rockwell, 49, pled guilty to one count of grand theft and one count of computer crime and agreed to pay restitution ordered by the court. The Idaho Attorney General's Office spelled out the bill: $176,300.29

wrongfully taken from the foundation, $58,291.60 in statutory interest, and $6,200 for forensic accounting services, as well as bank fees to obtain records. The total came to $241,289.89.

The IAGO, presumably, wanted all of it. The foundation wanted a bit more, claiming the amount wrongfully taken was "no less than $185,000." The forensic accounting turned up no evidence of big purchases by young Mrs. Rockwell during the spree. No shopping trips to New York City, no new Jag, Gucci bag, or Versace glad rag. Conclusion: the money went for ordinary household expenses. She spent $176,300.29—or "no less than $185,000"—on ordinary household expenses? That's a lot of milk and peanut butter, you heard Grangeville people say. And her husband, a financial advisor, didn't notice?

A citizen of nearby Cottonwood, in a letter to the *Free Press*, put the question this way:

> Idaho County has a proverbial elephant in its china closet. Apparently no one has the public courage to acknowledge it. Laurie Rockwell, wife of County Commissioner James Rockwell, has pleaded guilty to felony theft from our public hospital's foundation. Press reports on the matter have thus far been so cryptic they could pass as a deliberate attempt to suppress general knowledge of the felonies. The favor of an 'esteemed' reputation apparently has its value, broken china notwithstanding. [. . .] How is it possible, absent in situ birth, that elephant came to be inside the china shop? After all, it simply is not possible that the elephant entered via a standardized door, at least not without notice. Given that Mr. Rockwell's profession (and his public office) is one of fiduciary responsibility, how is it possible he did not know these significant sums of unaccounted monies entered his own household? Worse, why did the accountant and tax preparer fail to know? It is therefore fair to conclude that either Mr.

Rockwell has (a) not been forthright about his knowledge of that elephant or (b) he is grossly inferior to the requirements of his profession and public office. In either case, Mr. Rockwell should resign as county commissioner. Might I suggest instead, Barnum and Bailey?"

WHAT MICHELE AND I NOTICED was our garden greening up. Back in May when my rototiller wouldn't start, I used a spade to prepare the soil—the same method I used as a boy in my parents' backyard garden. It felt good, pushing the spade in with my foot, lifting and turning over the blade full of black, wormy, compost-enriched dirt. The tomatoes, lettuce, spinach, chard, beets, parsley, oregano, mint, rosemary—everything was properly showing off.

Weekdays, we drove to town for the noon lap-swim. We crawled up and down the lanes with Pauline, Judy, Mary (who was doing the "egg-beater" that summer) and, if he missed the seven A.M. lap-swim, Judge Jeff Payne, who married us. Between the two lap hours, Ciara and her crew of instructors gave lessons to children. The kids ranged from toddlers, who started out in the shallow end in the arms of a parent to get used to this big water, to the sprouts not yet worried by any sharp existential or ontological problems. Michele and I usually arrived at the pool a little early and were often reminded of those existential/ontological problems we all face, sooner or later, as we make our way trying to stay intact.

Reviewing certain points, for example, Ciara regularly held Q and A sessions in the shallow end with youngsters advanced enough to "make your bubbles" and stay afloat. Question: "We're on the ocean, our boat has sunk, and now we're in the water— what do we do first?" Answer (in unison): "Form two circles, little kids in the middle!" Question (to a boy in the middle circle): "Jonah, what do we do if we see a shark?" Jonah (quickly): "I'd get out!" Good man, Jonah, I'm with you.

BACK IN APRIL, A NEIGHBOR of the Rockwells, outside working
on his deck, could see across the field separating their properties
that James was outside, too, operating an excavator in his back
yard. "Hey, Louise," he called in to his wife, "James Rockwell is
digging a grave." She said, "What?" He repeated the comment.
"Oh, stop it," she chided him.

A popular explanation developed regarding how Laurie
was able to slip around her board of directors. First, the foundation, like the hospital, kept track of its own monies; unlike
the hospital, it did not have an accountant watching out for
mischief. Add to that Laurie's habit of holding only three or four
meetings a year. She would send out a memo saying that the
few items on their agenda were not worth a meeting and she
would take care of them. Like filing the annual IRS Reporting
and Disclosure documents required for tax-exempt status—
which she ignored. The board trusted Laurie with tax matters
because, after all, she worked part-time in her husband's E.K.
Riley office and knew about such things. But it wasn't only tax
matters they trusted her with: they trusted her in all matters—
completely. Plus, she had that knockout smile.

James Rockwell did not have her winning smile. Tall and
thin, he smiled, you could hazard, with real intent to make the
smile's recipient feel at ease and perhaps even like the smiler;
but what emerged above James's shiny jaw emerged, much like
his overall manner, a bit on the thin, stiff side. His wife's smile
was spontaneous and generous; his was guarded, as if the
tobacco under his lip might slip a little. Copenhagen, I thought,
didn't quite fit a rep-tie and tasseled-shoe kind of guy, but for
years he had the habit, despite his father, he said, warning him
against it many, many times.

He sat, that April day, at the controls of his little runabout
excavator and dug what certainly seemed to be a burial plot,
the neighbor thought. And it was. And it was intended for Dr.

Rockwell, who died at home on 25 April 2012, the same day Blanche Rockwell's letter about standing with him in support of Laurie appeared in the *Free Press.* He was 88. James obtained a variance from the city to bury the respected doctor in his own backyard, with the proviso that if the Rockwells moved, they had to dig the good man up and take with.

Would Blanche one day lie beside her husband in this very small cemetery? Would James land there? Laurie? Anyone else? Would the time come when the last Rockwell heirs did not want the property, preferring to sell it, and thus faced the chore of removing all those dusry remains?

I used to see Dr. Rockwell on the White Bird Battlefield walking the breaks. Walking the breaks—what a large, rich, wonderful phrase. (Perfect for describing the art of writing.) A dozen miles directly south of Grangeville, the Battlefield is rangy, rippled, grassy, open to a vast sky, and cluttered by nothing; it feels and smells natural because it is all-natural, basically undisturbed since the fray that named it. Few people go there— retired physicians fingering their rosaries, poets conjuring their lines, and, letting her dog run loose, a woman who had known the White Bird cowboy.

White Bird Battlefield of the Nez Perce National Historical Park—its full name—spreads out next to the little town of White Bird: 1,245 acres of hills and meadows and draws and ponds, plus 655 scenic easement acres—and all of it rising and falling. This was where a small band of Nez Perce, armed mainly with bows and arrows, were waiting. Waiting to be punished for some mayhem got up and fueled largely by temporal and spiritual greed—by a mix of squabbling Christian missionaries, gold, railroad expansion, and land on which the Nez Perce (a peaceful people who in 1806 saved Lewis and Clark's bacon) had lived for a long time.

A rift developed between those who wanted to keep to their land and traditional ways and those who favored the missionaries and a reservation. The latter signed a treaty that angered the former, including the lyrically named Toohoolhoolzote and White Bird. Indians were assassinated and some young Nez Perce men, heated up, struck back. Now they waited in that rising and falling geography to be punished. General Oliver O. Howard, upon dispatching the punishers, telegraphed his commander in San Francisco: "Think we will make short work of it." Two companies of US Cavalry arrived on 17 June 1877, almost a year to the day following Custer's defeat at Little Big Horn. Under a white flag, the Nez Perce walked out to meet them, hoping to discuss matters. Several soldiers opened fire. The Indians took out one of the cavalry's two buglers; their means of communication cramped, the punishers quickly became a confused mess, and the Nez Perce, who knew the territory, taught the army a lesson. The army lost thirty-four men, the Nez Perce none.

When Dr. Rockwell's Parkinson's no longer allowed him to negotiate the breaks, I would see him in the Grangeville Centennial Library reading the newspapers. We would nod to each other. He was tall and thin, of dignified bearing, with little hair and, some days, a little drool on his chin that he eventually caught up with and wiped away with his hand. One time a man in the library, near us, was on his cell phone. Loudly. He was visiting in the area and trying to locate, call after call, old acquaintances. I approached him. Would he mind taking his cell outside?

"Why?" he demanded.

"This *is* a library," I said.

"Oh! Oh! Well, holy shit, a library in big old Grangeville! Excuse *me*!"

The man stormed off. Dr. Rockwell seemed stunned, trying to say something. Finally he managed, with gravity, "Yes, this *is*, after all, a library."

He was buried in James and Laurie's backyard on a sunny May Saturday. A great many showed up at the visitation of the body on Willowrock Drive and for the rosary in Sts. Peter and Paul Church; fewer showed up—invitation only—at the burial. James's neighbor, who had observed the event across the field between them, said that after the priest finished with his last sprinkle of holy water over the casket, colored balloons were released into the air.

WHEN THE END CAME TO Laurie Rockwell's spree, it came in three parts: one, there was no more real money to withdraw; two, her board, becoming less trusting by the minute, was asking questions it had never asked her before; and three, Laurie took off running.

ON MY KNEES PLANTING A new crop of lettuce, I remember something, farmer-dreamer-thief that I am, and "Spring Evenings" begins in my head:

> Growing up in Flint I turned the dirt
> with a spade in our family's garden
> while my sister Gloria watched the baby
> and the baby, on bowed, rubbery legs
> watched our dad roll his eyes and wink
>
> leaning on his rake. Mother was the one
> who got this going, at the back door
> wiping her hands on her apron and warning
> we didn't have much time left—"Everything's
> almost ready." I love this homely scene
>
> I can't hold still. Fifty years later—
> that first garden long gone, Dad too, and last

fall my sister, who looked up from her usual morning
toast and coffee to say something funny
was going on—I turn the dirt in the raised beds

on my Idaho mountain: there's Mother again
wiping her hands, and there's Dad, almost
falling over, making the baby dance and laugh,
though what I'm smiling at are Gloria's
last words working to keep something

alive. Which is why we can't just quit
and go in right away, right? Why we can't
help helping ourselves to a little more,
never mind that it's so small
we can only get lost in it.

THE DRAMA TIGHTENED AS SENTENCING time got closer. Would
money talk? James's political connections in a cherry-red state?
Would privilege once again get away with a crime that com-
moners would damn well pay for? But the favored, in this case,
were already paying, no? Whatever the sentence, wasn't it hard
for the Rockwells to walk in public like they used to? As for the
backyard burial, was that paranoia, a circling of the wagons?

THE SKY OVER OUR PART of the Idaho panhandle became very
smoky that late August from a wildfire in central Washington
and Idaho fires south and east of us. I was reminded of the
major fire that threatened us in 2005. Planes and helicopters
dropping red retardant and water, smoke jumpers and hotshots
landing, pushing back the flames. Margaret and I had been to
dinner in Kamiah an hour away and driving home after dark
across the prairie we could see a bright red glow in the mountains
close to our place. I knew it was a fire. I also knew we still
needed at least thirty minutes to get home, where Margaret's
puppy, Saffy, was waiting for us. To delay anxiety and fear as

long as possible, I said, calmly, "Well, an interesting reflection over there." Margaret chewed on that "reflection" for about three beats, then said, "That's not any *reflection!* That's a *fire!*" She was eleven and loved her little dog waiting in the run beside the barn, so I drove faster than was wise on that winding two-lane.

Two miles from our house the police had set up a roadblock, turning cars back. This was on the Mount Idaho Grade, the hard surface road that led to our gravel road that in turn led to our driveway up to the house. I told the deputy where we lived, about the dog. He glanced at Margaret. He said, "Be quick." At the gravel road another deputy stopped us. I repeated what I'd told the first one. He said, "Five minutes. *Five.*" At the house, Saffy ran straight for the pickup and jumped in the back seat. In the house, I had baseballs signed by Ted Williams and Bob Feller, plus a card collection that included Al Kaline, Ernie Banks, Roberto Clemente, many others. If I could have put my hands on this stuff without breaking stride, I'd have taken it. But all I brought from the house were one eleven-year-old, her pillow, blanket, and toothbrush, and a bottle of my sweet well water that I kept in the fridge. My mouth was very dry.

In the pickup, Margaret sat with her pillow under one arm, Saffy under the other. I drove back down the mountain through a sharp, smoky stuffing everywhere in the darkness.

JUST BEFORE THAT 2005 FIRE, the Rockwells got involved in a hot legal drama—or so James's flushed face suggested whenever he mentioned it to me. I learned of this drama one day running into him on the street. I asked how things were going, not having seen him in a while, and he said great, that he and Laurie just got back from Detroit where they were "pursuing justice" in court. A former partner in Vietnam, he said, owed them money. I assumed he was referring to the glove factory, said something to that effect, and he nodded. Over the next year or so I'd see James on the street, and he'd say, getting a little excited in the telling, "Just back from Detroit. Big stuff." "The trial still going on?" "You bet." But he offered no details.

He and Laurie were in Hanoi from 1992 to 1998. According to Christopher W. Runckel—a former US diplomat in Asia who has called James Rockwell "a longtime friend"— [James was] "the first US businessman to receive a license by the Vietnamese government to operate a business in Vietnam (a license for consulting and later trading) . . ." When President Bill Clinton lifted the US Embargo with Vietnam in March 1993, James was on site, US and Vietnamese flags hanging side by side in his office, ready to deal as VATICO (Vietnam American Trade and Investment Consulting Co.).

In April 1994, court records show, he entered into an agreement with Hughes Aircraft to serve as Hughes's nonexclusive sales rep for the sale of an air traffic control system to Vietnam. Either party could terminate the agreement upon thirty days' written notice and ninety days after termination no commissions would be paid. In 1997 Hughes merged with Raytheon. Raytheon decided it no longer needed James's services, so in 1998 he was cut loose, and the Rockwells came home. The next year Raytheon sold a radar and flight-data-processing system to Vietnam.

In 2004 the Rockwells sued Raytheon-Hughes, saying they were owed a commission on that 1999 sale. James says he made a deal with the Vietnamese, prior to 1996, regarding those systems; essential terms were agreed upon; all that was left to do, the Vietnamese said to James, he said, was obtain financing. Nothing was in writing.

The court dismissed the Rockwells' lawsuit for lack of evidence long before the case came even close to a trial. They appealed. The Michigan Court of Appeals sent the case back down to allow the Rockwells to produce evidence which would support a claim to compensation, but not before commenting on how unlikely that prospect appeared. By the end of 2006, James and Laurie agreed to dismiss the case. The court's docket indicates only that the case "settled." There was no victory. On Main Street in Grangeville, however, James said to me, "We won. But we'll never see any money." A rare gloomy remark. But the fact was, their lawsuit was a fizzle.

It wouldn't be all that long before Laurie began withdrawing money from the Syringa Hospital Foundation accounts.

I WAS BEGINNING TO WONDER ABOUT all the time I was spending on the Rockwell story. Was it *that* interesting? *That* new? Lots of people in positions to do so will embezzle. From the privileged on down. They have a gambling problem. A sex-drive problem. A drug habit. Resentment. One day, perhaps accidentally, they push a button that results in an opportunity—whoa—that *no one* would know about. The head becomes lit up with, well, lightness, the tongue turns more than a smidgen dry, the eyes widen. A worm has crawled intimately into the scene—a nice-looking worm, actually—and our lit-up citizen, who is really, truly not a *real* thief yet, cannot help but hug it a tiny bit. You cute little worm, since you are already in my lap, let's have a kiss.

Anyway, our thief who is not a thief yet, just morally flexible, has that quick money and spends it. She/he, standing taller, thinks, "I deserve this." Time goes by. Hey, just for fun, let's see if that wrong button works again. Bingo, it does! Bagable money! A rush of blood to the face. Game's on.

The Rockwell story held my interest because I knew Laurie and James, and thinking about them called up Tolstoy's famous line that all happy families are alike but an unhappy family is unhappy after its own fashion. Moreover, the players in this

story occupied the kind of stage—stretching from one end of
Grangeville to the other—that only a small town can support.
Though many citizens declared, "I am so sick of that Rockwell
business," they still had something to say. "The judge will
sentence her to a couple of years, then suspend them. Give
her probation, *maybe* some community service. Is that right?"
The ladies volunteering at the hospital thrift shop—a steady
source of foundation income—were quietly appalled but, like
a Greek chorus, seethingly in tune: "We want our money back."
My neighbor Fred, a law-and-order man, even he could not
abandon the story to a temporal authority: "She's such a nice
person, every Sunday I pray she doesn't have to do jail time."

ORIGINALLY, LAURIE'S RESTITUTION HEARING AND sentencing
dates, respectively, were 27 July and 21 September 2012. Her
attorney requested a postponement—it was granted—moving
her new dates to 21 September and 4 October. On the morning
of 21 September, however, Judge Jeff Brudie, who had driven
down from Lewiston to preside, announced in District Court
in Grangeville the case against Laurie Rockwell would be
continued because the Rockwells had just produced checkbooks,
receipts, and credit-card statements that they felt would modify
the amount of money she allegedly stole. The state had received
these documents at 8 P.M. the previous night and needed time
to examine them, Judge Brudie said. Then Laurie's attorney,
Tom Clark, who also came down from Lewiston, asked to speak.
Judge Brudie told him to go ahead. Barely audible, Clark spoke
at length about his client's wish for that day's hearing to be
held as scheduled because she fervently wanted a speedy
conclusion to this case. During what many in the courtroom
viewed as Clark's disingenuous commercial, Judge Brudie,
glancing at him once or twice, shuffled papers. After Clark finally
sat down, Judge Brudie said he would announce the new

restitution and sentencing dates later. I heard someone in back of the courtroom stage whisper, "Now she'll get to be home for Christmas."

One month earlier, on 22 August, James Rockwell sent a letter to Judge Brudie, saying, "Here are the facts." James distributed copies of the letter to the IAGO, to Tom Clark, and to a number of citizens in the community; copies of the latter copies found, as they were bound to, a wider audience.

The five-page, single-space letter starts with James saying he supports and loves his wife. Then, "On or about the night of February 2, 2011, my wife called my brother in a state of high distress. She told him she had taken $58,500 from the Syringa Hospital Foundation. She asked him for money to repay the hospital. She told my brother not to tell me. She told him she had decided to kill herself. My brother called me in the morning, told me the story, told me to find my wife as she would not make it through the next twenty-four hours. I was at the office and raced home." He finds her car and her foundation files and computers gone, he says. He searches for her, makes phone calls. "Nothing for 20 hours." Then, "I awoke to find Laurie on our sofa, bedraggled and unkempt. She'd spent the day and night in Riggins contemplating death. I had her tell me the story. She did."

The letter goes on in this melodramatic way, demanding to know, in a refrain, "Where's the money?" He reports asking the IAGO's chief investigator, Scott Birch, where he thought it went— on drugs? gambling? family? He says Birch "said something to the effect that the only thing they could figure was that she spent the money on clothing and lattes." "Ridiculous," James writes. "Laurie drank two lattes a day and owns a total of 15 pair[s] of pants, half of which she bought at the Syringa Hospital Thrift Shop (sic) for $1 each."

He says or implies that the money she allegedly stole (he ups the state's figure to $179,000) was spent to "outfit" the hospital's clinics in Grangeville and Kooskia, plus "the new VA Clinic," and on items like cupcake holders, shotguns, Christmas wreaths, wine, meat, M&M'S, hotel rooms, vacations, paintings, flowers, Frisbees, and bottled water for such events as the Border Days rodeo and parade, the Festival of Trees, the Firecracker Run, and the Health Fair. He attributes her legal problems to "lousy" bookkeeping by the "go-to girl [who] was expected to make things happen." (He himself, he notes, "keep[s] an impeccable check register.") In addition to being a bad bookkeeper, she was "mentally ill." Then he says, "Dishonest? Nah. Stupid? Yes. Someone in a position of authority at the hospital should have questioned it." What he means by "it" is not clear, though the little pronoun seems to stand for pretty much everything that got her into this mess—bad bookkeeping, mental illness, and, last but not least, stupidity.

Bad bookkeeping, illness, and stupidity, however, are only commercials here; the feature presentation is the accusation aimed at "[s]omeone in a position of authority"—presumably the hospital's CEO, Joe Cladouhos—who should have been watching, as if the foundation were simply one more department in the hospital, like the lab or the ER, which was not the case. The foundation and the hospital were separate entities, though having a single chain of command up which to pass along ultimate blame for sloppy shopkeeping would serve James—and Laurie, too, of course—much better.

As for Laurie's guilty plea, James says, "On 13 medications, including lithium, after 14 months of waiting, faced with the specter of 10 felony charges from the attorney general, scared and mentally unstable, Laurie plead guilty to 2 felonies. She didn't ask for the plea bargain. The AG made the offer, but only after describing in years a 10 count life in prison." James implies that his wife went up against the AG all by herself. He leaves out that her attorney, Tom Clark, was representing her all the way in the negotiations and cut the best deal she could get.

James concludes his letter to Judge Brudie, "I think it is incumbent on the hospital and the prosecution to recognize the mental illness, to prove that unreceipted purchases were criminal, and to prove that money is in fact missing. I want truth. I ask for justice for my wife."

Does such a letter call up the spoiled noises of a child who usually got his way in a family to which the town gave plenty of room? The combative rant of a child who usually did not get his way and is still brooding about it? Who dropped out of college and learned how to sway large numbers of voters—plus carried the phone numbers of important players next to his heart? Who, with those credentials in his blazer pocket, should really be in charge of—of what? Whose political ambitions were now in an awful state? Who, lacking wit, likely misses the bitter irony of his wife disappearing on Ground Hog Day after seeing a long, cold winter ahead?

Judge Brudie ordered Laurie Rockwell and the attorney general's office to the mediation table. This meeting resulted in an agreement—reached after three hours—that Laurie would pay the Foundation $114,793 plus interest. Thus the $58,500 figure that she had confessed (to James's brother) stealing was almost doubled, and the $176,300 that the state said it found missing was reduced by a little over sixty thousand. Neither side was happy, which is usually taken as a successful mediation. The foundation expressed relief that the ordeal was over, and presumably a measure of relief was felt in the Rockwell keep.

Laurie agreed to pay $15,000 right away and $500 a month until the full bill—principal and interest—was paid. Some wondered why she (and James) didn't just cough up the full amount now? Show the community that she (they) wanted to make nice ASAP? James had claimed in his 22 August letter to Judge Brudie that he earned "in excess of $100,000 per year," and before that publicly announced he would immediately pay back every cent his wife stole—why couldn't he make restitution happen bingo-bango? Or had too many big changes come to the Rockwells, including a somewhat ironic new sign on James's place of business? *Summit* had replaced *E.K. Riley*. Had James, though linguistically elevated, been lowered? Plus, the IRS would have an interest in this matter. And the bill from Tom Clark, Laurie's attorney, would likely eat up the major portion of James's yearly earnings, if not all of it.

On 6 December 2012, in front of a full courtroom audience, including her five children, her husband, and her mother-in-law, Judge Brudie sentenced Laurie Rockwell. But first he allowed some final witnesses. Darla Anglen-Whitley, the foundation's new executive director, took the stand and cited figures showing that donations following allegations against Laurie Rockwell had fallen by fifty per cent. She said donors were angry, volunteers quitting, board members resigning. The hospital's CEO, Joe Cladouhos, said that at the rate of $500 a month it would take Laurie Rockwell thirty-five years to pay off her debt. "Is this another example of a good deal for the defendant?" He pointed out that during the period of her thefts she was being paid about $138,000 by the hospital, plus benefits, for her part-time position—while also working in her husband's stockbroker office.

In Laurie's behalf Lynn Fraley, a mental health counselor, spoke via a conference call from her office in Moscow. "It's a shame," she said, "that it took [the thefts] to reveal her manic depression." A woman, who described herself as Laurie's best friend, said, "I love her and her family." A farmer said he had seen the Rockwells at least once a week for seventeen years and thought that Laurie was "a loving mother and valuable member of the community." Then James was sworn in.

Still standing, facing the judge, he started to speak. Judge Brudie told him to sit down in the witness chair, which seemed to surprise James. The position of the witness chair encouraged its occupant to face the audience, but James wanted the judge's attention—man to man, his tone and manner said, they'd get this matter taken care of—and sat sideways, on the edge of the chair, which made him appear somewhat foolish. "Christmas is a good time," he began again, "to understand the true nature of family." Not for the first time, I thought that James would really like to be some important prelate's wisest adviser.

When James finished his speech, Assistant Attorney General Jason Spillman asked him three times, with slightly different phrasing, if it was James's sworn testimony that his wife had *hidden* her criminal activity from him until 3 February 2011— the date on which James said he "asked her to tell me the story." Three times James answered, "Yes." These were the only questions Jason Spillman had for any of the witnesses, and it was the first time in this long case against Laurie Rockwell that James had put himself in a potentially perjurious position.

Then Judge Brudie sentenced Laurie to what the state had asked for: two years fixed, up to twelve and fourteen years indeterminate, respectively, on the two counts she had pled guilty to, to be served concurrently in the women's penitentiary in Boise. At that moment, Laurie, sitting beside Tom Clark, her back to the hundred or so citizens come to see justice or a forgiving angel, seemed to clench. She bent forward, her hands gripped in a posture of prayer. She wore her black hair in a bun, and the bun bobbed. Then Judge Brudie suspended that sentence to seven months in the Idaho County Jail, located just a few doors down the hall from where we all sat. Outside, the marquee thermometer scrolling over the entrance to Irwin

Drugs on Main Street had dropped close to freezing, but in the packed courtroom it was warm enough to bring out a flush on many faces. Then Judge Brudie lopped thirty days off the seven months. But he wanted Laurie to know she had brought real harm to a town that once trusted her. It was unlikely, he said, his voice rising to a level of sharpness that no priest in his pulpit could thrust more deeply into the heart of a miscreant mother in front of her most precious issue, that she would never be so trusted again.

She would report to the county jailor by five P.M. on Friday, 14 December.

THE *FREE PRESS,* ON ITS editorial page, wrote: "Certainly, no recent crime has been of such interest and regional impact as the case of Laurie Rockwell, who [. . .] stole thousands of dollars of—and let's be clear on this—the time, generosity and hard work of county residents, patients, volunteers and hospital staff." It went on: "We're not at all pleased with the restitution settlement that allows $500 monthly payments for the next three decades." The editorial echoed the talk around town: "[T]aking out a loan to pay the balance would have been a good start at reconciliation . . ." A letter from a citizen called the restitution payment plan "preposterous!" The citizen also said that James "must have known something was going on." An opinion that many in Grangeville seemed to have formed long ago.

ON 25 JANUARY 2015, ALMOST four years to the day Laurie Rockwell left home in a panic and her husband said he could not find her, some children were playing around a waning cabin on an old homestead property on the Salmon River in Keuterville, less than an hour's drive from Grangeville. Exploring the cabin, one of the children found and showed her father a "package wrapped in black plastic and secured with black duct or Gorilla-type tape," the office of Idaho County Sheriff Doug Giddings said. The wrapping was cut through and "inside was a red velvet-lined jewelry type of box" packed with cash money. The riverfront property was owned by Salmon Canyon Ranch, a limited liability corporation (LLC) formed in 2010; its registered agent was James Rockwell.

Members of the LLC were immediately contacted, the *Free Press* reported, and they "disavowed any knowledge regarding the money, which was then turned over to the sheriff."

The packaging and money were sent to the state lab for fingerprint detection and the Federal Reserve was asked to identify, via serial numbers, which financial institutions the bills were shipped to.

"Who left a sealed container of tens of thousands of dollars at a remote Keuterville property, and why?" the *Free Press* asked.

A man named George Brown showed up at Giddings's office and demanded the money. It was his, he said. Brown and his wife, formerly residents of Washington state, were now living in Grangeville in the old family home of Dr. and Mrs. Rockwell. Mrs. Brown was a sister of James Rockwell. Her husband, according to court records, was being sued by creditors, including a foreclosure on land in Idaho County. Brown paid several visits to Giddings's office demanding his money.

Three months later the Federal Reserve Bank of San Francisco notified Giddings's office that the $100 bills in that jewelry-type box had been shipped to banks in Tacoma and Renton, Washington, in December 2013 and January 2014, respectively. Giddings turned the money over to Brown.

"The money didn't connect to anything or anybody," the sheriff said. "This is my job to make sure, and we did that." As for why Brown stored the money where he did, the *Free Press* said, "Giddings declined to elaborate, referring inquiry to Brown who is currently unavailable."

A report from the state lab regarding fingerprint identification still had not arrived in Grangeville.

LET'S GET SOME FRESH AIR. The sweet and thoughtful, the arrogant and cunning, the meek, greedy, hard-working, lazy, long-suffering, hopeful, pious, shy, proud, loud, wholly together, cheerful, bad, bold, and generous will continue, as will the nitwits who get to be in charge for a while. Walter J. Hickel, a former governor of Alaska, became, briefly, secretary of the interior. Friendly to developers eager to get at Alaska's mineral and timber holdings, Hickel said, "We can't just let nature run wild." President Nixon, who appointed him and could have used a jester, fired the man many called a clown. Hickel was not a clown. Red Skelton and Emmett Kelly were clowns. They reminded us of our membership in a fragile humanity and our ability to laugh at ourselves. Hickel was altogether something else.

Closer

I had recently moved to northern Idaho to write, and everything I wrote was dull, forced, unnatural. One day I saw a cougar. He was easily eight feet, from his tawny head to the tip of his long tail lazily rising and falling, about the same size as the trophy cougar I once saw displayed in a glass box at a gas station down in Kamiah. He lay stretched out on pine needles on a slope forty yards away. I felt lucky to have seen him. I was also glad to be inside my house; we had come close enough.

The house I bought sits amid thousands of acres of timber in the Clearwater Mountains, high above the South Fork of the Clearwater River. The day after seeing the cougar, I decided to take down a hog-wire fence from a wooded area where the previous owners kept small livestock. I had no interest in raising anything there; I wanted what came forth on its own urges—deer, blackberries, turkeys, dogtooth violets—to have free play. Working around a thicket of wild roses to loosen the fence, I saw the bright carcass of a six-point buck. Something had been eating it. From the fresh scratch marks on a fallen larch holding up the buck's rack, I knew it was the cougar.

I once asked a forest ranger what I should do if I was ever surprised by one in the woods. "Likely the lion would see you first," he said. "And if he really wanted to jump you and break your neck, you'd probably never even feel it. Or," he added, "not long enough to worry about."

Charley Dreadfulwater, who has worked in these mountains for thirty years, helps me with chores I don't dare try on my own, like dropping big trees dangerously close to my barn. I told him about the kill. You don't know what to think about lions anymore, he said. "Used to be, you'd never see them, just their markings," he said. "Now their fear seems to be gone. Last month, out after firewood, I had three of them not sixty feet away looking me over. Calm as anything. I eased back into my truck and waited for them to go away. I like lions. They were here first." He shook his head. "But there's only so much land."

A week later, I went to check on the kill. Only a rag of its fur, its bones and hooves remained. Charley told me that since I wasn't a hunter, which deer figure out pretty quickly, I'd always have plenty close by. And something to eat them. For several days, I avoided walking in the woods near dusk, when the cougar could see better than I could. But I kept staying out later and later, my neck aching from looking into low branches perfect for leaping from. Was I going crazy? Did I want to see a lion perched in a tree, waiting for me? Why didn't I at least buy a pistol?

One afternoon about a month later, I was in the corral, on my knees, pulling up thistles. The cold air was misty wet from a low cloud. I was trying to work off the bad feeling of having made mediocre sentences all morning. It seemed I was becoming an expert. I thought how my dad, a carpenter, could caress the grain in wood and just about make the wood sing. What would he think of his son's courting self-pity?

As the mist shifted, the Gospel Hump Mountains came into view. I loved how the clouds seemed to rub their pearly gray peaks into another season. What happened next is hard to explain exactly. I looked up and saw the cougar. He stood in the mist curled around us, close enough to touch, not moving. We looked at each other. Over his shoulder, I could see Gospel Peak covered with snow. Part of me wanted nothing more than to lie in the snow on the peak, slowly move my arms and make a great angel. I also wanted my father to be alive again and see this magnificence with me—we wouldn't have to say anything. I just wanted to hold his hand.

I was quite afraid—even to blink—but also calm. I wanted to see my father shake his head in wonder, the way he did after finishing a tough job, when he had to admit he was happy. Because if I moved, surely my heart would escape and fly off.

How long the cougar stayed I don't know. I remember how clear everything was—the pointy buds on my plum trees, his eyes, the dark whorls the knots made in the boards of my fence. And that perfect, priceless silence in his wake when he turned and went back, as smoothly it seemed as a trout in water.

Years have passed. I have not seen him—or any kills—so close again. Charley smiled when I told him about our meeting. "Maybe he figured this is your hunting ground."

Once upon a time, a big lion suddenly showed up and might have hurt me, or worse, but instead left me with a sharpened way of looking. I can see great distances—rain falling in fat columns miles away while the sun warms my bare shoulders. I can hear great distances too. A pine cone dropping branch by branch—*pwak! pwak!* Or the sudden flutter of a chukar's wings. When the two senses come together, it's often stunning. Moonlit nights, standing at my window, I can see a passage of the South Fork's curled brilliance that sounds like a woman removing and collecting in her hand a long strand of favored pearls.

Gary Gildner has given readings at the 92 St. Y, Manhattan Theatre Club, Library of Congress, Shakespeare & Co. in Paris, and on the ferry crossing Lake Michigan. He's been writer-in-residence at Reed, Davidson, and Randolph colleges, Seattle University, and Michigan State. Among his many books are two memoirs, a novel, four collections of stories and eight of poems. He and Michele have traded the Clearwater Mountains of Idaho for the foothills of the Catalina Mountains of Arizona.

BkMk Press is grateful for the support it has recently received
from the following organizations and individuals:

Missouri Arts Council
Miller-Mellor Foundation
Neptune Foundation
Richard J. Stern Foundation for the Arts
Stanley H. Durwood Foundation
William T. Kemper Foundation

Anonymous
Dwight Arn
Beverly Burch
Jaimee Wriston Colbert
Maija Rhee Devine
Charles Egan
Alice Friman
Elizabeth Goldring
Whitney and Mariella Kerr
Carla Klausner
Lorraine M. López
Patricia Cleary Miller
Deborah A. Miranda
Margot Patterson
Alan Proctor
James Hugo Rifenbark
Roderick and Wyatt Townley